Geeks On Call®
Security and Privacy

Geeks On Call® Security and Privacy

J. R. King

Wiley Publishing, Inc.

Geeks On Call® Security and Privacy: 5-Minute Fixes

Published by
Wiley Publishing, Inc.
10475 Crosspoint Boulevard
Indianapolis, IN 46256
www.wiley.com

Copyright © 2006 by Geeks On Call America, Inc., Norfolk, Virginia

Published by Wiley Publishing, Inc., Indianapolis, Indiana

Published simultaneously in Canada

ISBN-13: 978-0-471-77455-6
ISBN-10: 0-471-77455-3

Manufactured in the United States of America

10 9 8 7 6 5 4 3 2 1

1B/SY/RR/QV/IN

For general information on our other products and services or to obtain technical support, please contact our Customer Care Department within the U.S. at (800) 762-2974, outside the U.S. at (317) 572-3993 or fax (317) 572-4002.

Library of Congress Cataloging-in-Publication Data

King, J. R.
  Geeks On Call security and privacy : 5-minute fixes / J. R. King.
     p. cm.
  Includes index.
  ISBN-13: 978-0-471-77455-6 (pbk.)
  ISBN-10: 0-471-77455-3 (pbk.)
  1. Computer security. I. Title.
  QA76.9.A25K5426 2005
  005.8—dc22

                              2005026357

Wiley also publishes its books in a variety of electronic formats. Some content that appears in print may not be available in electronic books.

Credits

Executive Editor
Carol Long

Development Editor
Tom Dinse

Copy Editor
Nancy Rapoport

Editorial Manager
Mary Beth Wakefield

Production Manager
Tim Tate

Vice President and Executive Group Publisher
Richard Swadley

Vice President and Executive Publisher
Joseph B. Wikert

Project Coordinator
Michael Kruzil

Graphics and Production Specialists
Jennifer Heleine
Barbara Moore
Lynsey Osborn
Alicia B. South

Quality Control Technicians
Amanda Briggs
Carl William Pierce
Charles Spencer

Proofreading and Indexing
TECHBOOKS Production Services

Contents

Introduction   xiii

Part I: Windows Security   1

Chapter 1: Update Windows and Microsoft Office   3

Manually Update Windows   3
Automatically Update Windows (XP Home/Pro only)   6
Update Microsoft Office   7

Chapter 2: Safeguard Windows   13

Protect Your Computer While You're Temporarily Away   13
    Log Off   13
    Lock Windows   14
Prevent a Screensaver Hack (Windows XP Pro and
    Windows 2000 only)   14
Rename the Administrator Account (Windows XP Pro
    and Windows 2000 only)   17
Disable the Guest Account (Windows XP Home/Pro
    and Windows 2000 only)   19
Disable Remote Desktop (Windows XP Pro only)   20
Disable Remote Assistance (Windows XP
    Home/Pro only)   22
Disable File and Printer Sharing   23
Clear the Pagefile (Windows XP Home/Pro and
    Windows 2000 only)   25
Disable the Dump File (Windows XP Home/Pro and
    Windows 2000 only)   27
Disable Simple File Sharing (Windows XP Pro only)   28
Remove Web Servers   29
Modify the Hosts File   31
    Automatically   31
    Manually   31
Unhide File Extensions   34
Unhide Special Extensions   35
Disable VBScripts   36
Disable Messenger (Windows XP Home/Pro and
    Windows 2000)   40

Part II: E-Mail Security   43

Chapter 3: Protect Outlook Express   45

Enable Maximum Security   45
Disable the Preview Pane   46

Safely View E-Mail 47
Read E-Mail in Plain Text (Outlook Express 6 only) 48
Send E-Mail in Plain Text 49
View a Blocked E-Mail Attachment 49

Chapter 4: Protect Outlook 51

Download the Latest Security Patches and Service
    Packs for Microsoft Office 51
Disable the Preview Pane 51
Safely View E-Mail Details 52
Read E-Mail in Plain Text 52
Send E-Mail in Plain Text 55
Turn on Attachment Alerts 56

Part III: Digital Threats 57

Chapter 5: Viruses and Worms 59

Symptoms of Virus or Worm Infection 59
How Do Viruses Infect a Computer? 60
Protect Your Computer from Viruses 60
Antivirus Software 60
What Damage Can a Virus Do? 61
When to Update Your Antivirus Software 61
Protect Your Computer from Macro Viruses 61
How to Tell If a File Is Infected 62
If You Think Your Computer Is Infected with a Virus 62
    If You Have Antivirus Software Installed 62
    If You Don't Have Antivirus Software Installed 64
How Do Worms Infect a Computer? 64
What Damage Can a Worm Do? 64
Prevent Worms from Invading Your Computer 65
Disable the Preview Pane in Outlook and
    Outlook Express 65
If You Think Your Computer Is Infected with a Worm 66

Chapter 6: Spyware 67

Symptoms of Spyware Infection 67
How Does Spyware Infect a Computer? 68
What Does Spyware Do? 68
If You Think Your Computer Is Infected with Spyware 69
Anti-Spyware Programs 70
    Reactive Anti-Spyware Programs 70
    Proactive Anti-Spyware Programs 70

Chapter 7: Wireless Threats 71

Invisible Criminals 71
    Wi-Fi Hacking 71
    Evil Twin Hotspots 73

Invasion of the Data Snatchers   73
    Wireless Keyboards   74
    Cell Phones   74

Chapter 8: Phishing Scams   75

Gone Phishing   75
    Types of Phishing   75
    Warning Signs   76
    How to Avoid Phishing Scams   76
Phishy E-Mail   79
    How to Spot a Fake Microsoft E-Mail   79
    Examples of Fraudulent E-Mail   80

Chapter 9: Spam   85

    Canning Spam   85

Chapter 10: Cookies   87

    Are Computer Cookies Yummy?   87
    Trustworthy Cookies   87
    Tracking Cookies   87
How to Control Cookies   88
    Manual Deletion   88
    Web-Browser Tweaks   89
    Software Solutions   93

Part IV: Internet Security   95

Chapter 11: Safe Web Surfing   97

    Hardware Firewalls   98
    Software Firewalls   98
        Free Firewalls   98
        Retail Firewalls   99
    Don't Use Internet Connection Sharing   100
    Secure Your Router   100
    Surf Cautiously   100
    Block Pop-Ups   101
    Test Your Firewall   101
    Consider Other Browsers   102
Tweak Internet Explorer   102
    Create a Custom Security Level   103
    Add Trusted Sites   105
    Disable AutoComplete   107
    Block Cookies   108
    Configure Advanced Options   109
    Tweak Firefox   110

Chapter 12: Safe Instant Messaging   117

Chapter 13: Safe Chatting   119

Chapter 14: Safe E-Shopping   121

Chapter 15: Web Safety for Kids   123

Create Separate Accounts (Windows XP
Home/Pro only)   123
Establish Boundaries   124
Block Web Sites and Content   124
Use the Content Advisor   124
Content-Filtering Software   127
Follow Their Tracks   128
Teach Them Safe Chatting   129
Practice Safe Instant Messaging   129

Part V: Data Security   131

Chapter 16: Passwords and Privacy   133

Disable the Welcome Screen (Windows XP
Home/Pro only)   133
Require Secure Logon (Windows XP Pro and
Windows 2000 only)   134
Create Passwords for Windows Accounts
(XP Home/Pro and 2000 only)   135
Require a Password for Screensavers   137
Create a BIOS Password   137
Change Passwords for Other Hardware   138
Use Strong Passwords   138
Passwords to Avoid   139
Web Site Passwords   140
How to Remember All of Your Passwords   140
Prevent Your Windows Password from Being
Lost or Forgotten (XP Home/Pro only)   140
If You Forget Your Windows Password
(XP Home/Pro only)   141
If You Forget Your Primary Windows Password and
Don't Have a Password-Reset Disk
(XP Home/Pro only)   142
Remove the "Password Is About to Expire" Notice
(Windows XP Pro and Windows 2000 only)   143
Make Folders Private   145

Chapter 17: Data Deletion   149

Data Afterlife   149
What Happens When the Recycle Bin Is Emptied?   149
Delete Data Once and for All   150
Wiping Software   150

How to Safely Sell or Donate Your Computer 150
How to Wipe Your Computer 151
Properly Disposing of a Hard Drive 151
Properly Disposing of CDs, DVDs, Floppy Disks, and
Zip Disks 152

Chapter 18: Data Encryption 153

Deadbolt Your Data 153
Encryption Software 153
Windows Encryption (XP Pro and Windows 2000 only) 154
Encrypt a File 154
Encrypt a Folder 155
Give Encryption Permission (Windows XP
Pro only) 157
Encryption Tips (Windows XP Pro and
Windows 2000 only) 158
Encrypt the Temp Folder 158
Encrypt Offline Files (Windows XP Pro only) 160
Steganography 161

Chapter 19: Data Backup 163

Reasons to Back Up Your Computer Data 163
When to Back Up Your Data 164
Backup Devices 164
External Hard Drive 164
Internal Hard Drive 165
Recordable or Rewriteable CD/DVD Burners 165
RAID Your Computer 166
How to Copy Data to a Backup Device 166
Buy Burning Software from a Store 166
Use Windows XP 166
Backup Options 167
Manually Back Up Your Important Files 167
Create a Disc Image 168
Where to Store Backed-Up Data 168

Part VI: Privacy Protection 171

The Global Village 171

Chapter 20: Safely Use Public Computers 173

Be Private in Public 173

Chapter 21: Protect Laptops 177

Lock Down Your Laptop 177

Chapter 22: Identity Theft   179

Thwart Identity Thieves   179
Surf Anonymously   182
Guard Your Identity   183
If You Are a Victim of Identity Theft   183

Glossary   187

Index   191

Introduction

Welcome to the New Wild West

The expansion and populating of cyberspace is reminiscent of America's Old West (at least the version depicted in Hollywood films): Bad guys roam the landscape, lawlessness reigns, and heroes are desperately needed. Just when it seems as if all hope is lost, the cavalry charges to the rescue—but instead of riding horses, they drive blue Chrysler PT Cruisers. **Geeks On Call** is restoring order to this high-tech frontier by delivering on-site computer services to homes and businesses and by equipping computer users with knowledge to defend themselves from ruthless Internet threats. After all, safeguarding a computer nowadays is as much about establishing good habits as it is about installing protective software.

PART I

WINDOWS SECURITY

Why Do Bad Things Happen to Good Computers?

In recent years, you probably have seen news stories about security flaws discovered in the various versions of Microsoft's Windows operating system. Microsoft has always been quick to patch the holes, but that hasn't stopped some people from wondering why Microsoft makes a flawed product. A simple answer is that human beings aren't perfect and neither is anything they create. But there is a more important question that is often overlooked: Why do people continually search for cracks in Windows and then use them to break into computers? Some may do it for fun. Others do it to infect your computer with spyware that will display pop-up advertisements. Still others do it to access your private data, which they can use to commit identity theft. Regardless of their motives, these intruders must be stopped—and an easy way to do that is to update Windows and tweak its settings, which dramatically increases your safety.

1

UPDATE WINDOWS AND MICROSOFT OFFICE

Each summer, homeowners face an unenviable chore: painting and caulking their windows. True, this process is a hassle, but they know their efforts will keep out unwanted moisture and protect their investment. But glass windows aren't the only ones that require maintenance; their digital counterpart — Microsoft's Windows — also requires some virtual caulk to keep out unwanted intruders and protect private data from being stolen. Fortunately, this process is simple and mostly automated — and you won't have to spend forever trying to wash caulk off your hands.

Manually Update Windows

Over the years, Microsoft has released numerous security updates for every version of Windows. No matter if you use Windows XP, Windows 98, or anything in between, you must download the appropriate patches to ensure the safety of your computer. To do so, visit the Windows Update Web site.

1. Connect to the Internet.

2. Open Internet Explorer.

3. In the Address box, type **http://windowsupdate.microsoft.com** (see Figure 1-1).

Note
Do not type www in this Web address.

Do It Yourself

Manually update Windows

Automatically update Windows (XP Home/Pro only)

Update Microsoft Office

Figure 1-1

4. At the Windows Update Web site, you might be asked to install a small program that will help the site "talk" to your computer. Depending on your version of Windows, click the Yes or Install button (see Figures 1-2 and 1-3). When this process is finished, you will see the main page of the Windows Update site.

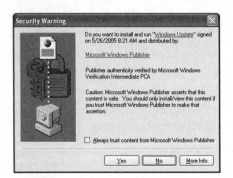

Figure 1-2

Figure 1-3

5. Depending on your version of Windows, click the Express: Get high-priority updates button (see Figure 1-4) or the Express Install: High-priority updates for your computer button.

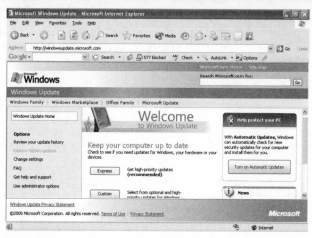

Figure 1-4

6. The Windows Update Web site scans your computer to determine which security patches are missing (see Figure 1-5). When the scan is finished, follow the onscreen instructions to download and automatically install the updates. It is recommended that you begin by downloading the *service packs*, which are critical collections of various patches and fixes.

Note

Not all security patches, updates, or service packs can be downloaded at the same time. You may need to return to the Windows Update Web site several times to retrieve all of them.

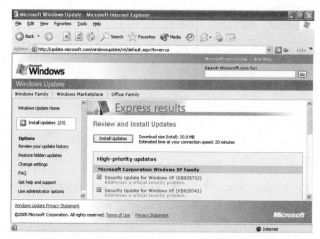

Figure 1-5

7. Once the updates have been installed, it is likely that you will be asked to restart your computer.

Create Shortcuts to Web Sites

After connecting to an important or frequently visited Web site such as Windows Update, create a shortcut known as a "bookmark" (also called a "favorite") to make it quick and easy to return to that site.

    a. If you use Internet Explorer, click the Favorites drop-down menu.

    b. Click Add to Favorites.

    c. A window opens. In the Name box, give the bookmark a name that will make it easy to identify.

    d. Next to the words Create In, select the folder in which you would like to save your bookmark. If you want to create a new folder to put your bookmark in, click the New Folder button, give the folder a name, and then click OK.

    e. After you have selected a folder to put the bookmark in, click OK to exit the Favorites window.

8. After your computer has rebooted, return to the Windows Update Web site as many times as necessary until all possible security patches and service packs have been downloaded and installed.

9. Turn on Windows XP's Automatic Updates feature as explained in the following fix to ensure that you never miss another critical update.

Automatically Update Windows (XP Home/Pro only)

To guarantee that your computer is always updated with the most recent Windows security patches, updates, and service packs, turn on automatic updates. Windows XP gives you three options: automatic download/install, download only, and notify only. Here's how to do it:

1. Right-click the My Computer icon on your desktop. If this icon is not available, then click the Start button in the lower-left corner of Windows and right-click My Computer. If you can't find the My Computer icon anywhere, do the following:

    a. Right-click in the empty space on your desktop.

    b. Select Properties.

    c. A window opens. Click the Desktop tab.

    d. Near the bottom of the window, click the Customize Desktop button.

    e. Another window opens. On the General tab, beneath the words Desktop Icons, select the My Computer checkbox.

    f. Click OK.

　　　g. You are returned to the previous screen. Click the Apply button.

　　　h. Click OK.

　　　i. The My Computer icon appears on your desktop. Right-click it.

2. Select Properties.

3. A window opens. Click the Automatic Updates tab.

4. On the Automatic Updates page, you have a choice (see Figure 1-6):

- For maximum protection, click the Automatic (recommended) button, which takes care of the updating silently behind the scenes. Use the two drop-down menus to select a day and time for Windows XP to search for updates and install them when necessary.

- If you would rather have more control over the updates that are installed on your computer, click the button Download updates for me, but let me choose when to install them. Another option is to click the button Notify me but don't automatically download or install them.

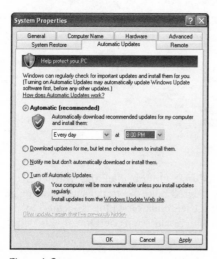

Figure 1-6

5. Click Apply.

6. Click OK.

Update Microsoft Office

Just like Windows, the Microsoft Office software — such as Word, Outlook, Excel, and PowerPoint — must be updated with the most recent security patches to protect it from digital threats and Internet criminals. No matter how old or new your Office programs are, you should visit the Office Update Web site every few months to see if new patches have been released.

Note

To install most Office updates, you need the MS Office CD-ROM that came with your computer or with your software purchase.

1. Connect to the Internet.

2. Open Internet Explorer.

3. In the Address box, type **http://office.microsoft.com** (see Figure 1-7).

Note

Do not type www in this Web address.

Figure 1-7

4. After connecting to Microsoft Office Online, click the words Check for Updates (usually they are located near the upper-right corner of the site). If you don't see them, then click Downloads located in the upper-left column of the site, which will open the Downloads page.

Note

To make it easy to find this Web page again, create a bookmark (also known as a "favorite") as described earlier in this chapter.

5. Click the words Check for Updates located in the left column below the words Things to Do (see Figure 1-8).

6. The Office Update Web site scans your computer to determine what security patches are missing (see Figure 1-9). If you are asked to download the Office Update Installation Engine, select Yes (see Figure 1-10).

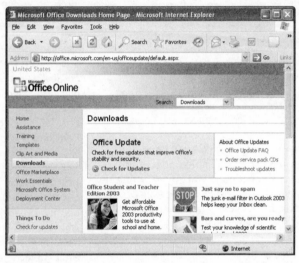

Figure 1-8

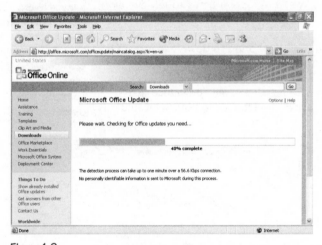

Figure 1-9

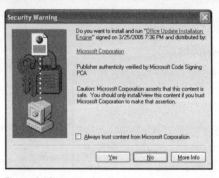

Figure 1-10

7. When the scan is complete, you will be able to scroll through the list of available updates and select the ones to download. Start by selecting the *service packs*, which are critical collections of various patches and fixes. Next, click the Agree and Install button (see Figure 1-11).

Note

Not all security patches, updates, or service packs can be downloaded at the same time. You may need to return to the Office Update Web site several times to retrieve all of them.

8. When you click the option to download a service pack, you may be whisked away to a separate Microsoft Web page, shown in Figure 1-12, that requires you to install a small "download assistant." If so, click the Download button located on the right side of this page.

FYI

When installing software over the Internet, you might see a pop-up window that asks you to always trust content or software from a particular company by placing a checkmark in the corresponding box. DO NOT do this. Checking this box allows that company to install software on your computer without asking for your permission each time, which means you will have no control over what is placed on your hard drive. Regardless of whether the company is Microsoft or an unknown organization, it is never a good idea to give anyone complete freedom to install programs on your computer at their discretion.

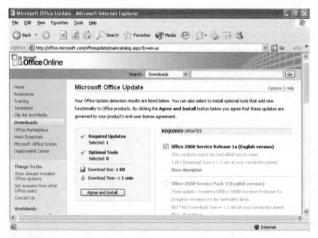

Figure 1-11

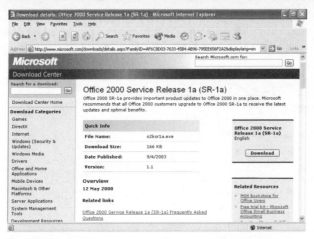

Figure 1-12

9. A window opens, and you are asked: Would You Like to Open the File or Save It to Your Computer? Click the Open button.

10. You are shown a license agreement. Click I Accept the Terms in the License Agreement.

11. Click Next.

12. In the next window, click the Update Office button (see Figure 1-13).

Figure 1-13

13. Click Next.

14. The download assistant will begin to transfer the service pack to your computer. Because of the large size of the download, this process could take an hour or more if you have a slow dial-up Internet connection. If you have a high-speed Internet connection, the process should take only a few minutes.

15. When the installation of the service pack begins, you probably will be asked to insert your Office CD-ROM into your computer's CD drive. Do so, and then click OK (see Figure 1-14). The installation will continue.

Figure 1-14

16. When the installation is finished, you will receive a message saying The Update Completed Successfully. Click OK.

17. Once the updates have been installed, it is likely that you will be asked to restart your computer.

18. Once your computer has rebooted, return to the Office Update Web site as many times as necessary until all possible security patches and service packs have been downloaded and installed.

2

SAFEGUARD
WINDOWS

*O*n the TV show *Extreme Makeover: Home Edition*, a team of construction experts blesses deserving families by tearing apart their old dwellings and rebuilding them into sleek, beautiful homes. In a similar way, you can make Windows more sleek and safe by giving it an extreme security makeover.

Protect Your Computer While You're Temporarily Away

If you need to step away from your computer for a few minutes, it could be vulnerable to intrusion by anyone who has physical access or Internet access to your system. Here is what to do to prevent this.

Log Off

The safest way to protect your computer while you are away is to log off. But be advised that logging off requires you to shut down all files, folders, and programs you are using, so save your work first.

For Windows XP Home Edition and XP Professional Edition
1. Click the Start button in the lower-left corner of Windows.
2. Click the Log Off button.
3. A window opens containing another Log Off button. Click it.

For Windows 2000
1. Click the Start button in the lower-left corner of Windows.
2. Click Shut Down.
3. In the drop-down menu, select Log Off.

Do It Yourself

Protect your computer while you're temporarily away

Prevent a screensaver hack (Windows XP Pro and Windows 2000 only)

Rename the administrator account (Windows XP Pro and Windows 2000 only)

Disable the Guest account (Windows XP Home/Pro and Windows 2000 only)

Disable Remote Desktop (Windows XP Pro only)

Disable Remote Assistance (Windows XP Home/Pro only)

Disable File and Printer Sharing

Clear the Pagefile (Windows XP Home/Pro and Windows 2000 only)

Disable the Dump File (Windows XP Home/Pro and Windows 2000 only)

Disable Simple File Sharing (Windows XP Pro only)

Remove Web servers

Modify the hosts file

Unhide file extensions

Unhide special extensions

Disable VBScripts

Disable Messenger (Windows XP Home/Pro and Windows 2000)

Alternate Shortcut for Windows XP Professional Edition and Windows 2000

For Windows XP Professional Edition, you must disable the "Welcome Screen" to use this shortcut. For more information, see the fix in Chapter 16 titled "Disable the Welcome Screen."

1. On your keyboard, press the Ctrl, Alt, and Delete keys simultaneously.

2. Select the option to Lock Computer.

Lock Windows

To avoid the hassle of closing your files and saving your work, you can choose to lock Windows XP instead of logging off.

For Windows XP Home Edition and XP Professional Edition

If your Keyboard has a Windows logo key (which looks like the Microsoft flag logo):

1. Press the Windows key and the L key together.

2. You are taken to the Welcome screen or to a log-in box (depending on whether or not your computer uses a feature called Fast User Switching).

3. To return to Windows, retype your password in the Welcome screen or log-in box.

If your keyboard does not have the Windows logo key but has Fast User Switching enabled:

1. Click the Start button in the lower-left corner of Windows.

2. Click the Log Off button.

3. Click the Switch User button.

4. To return to Windows, click your username and then type your password.

Prevent a Screensaver Hack (Windows XP Pro and Windows 2000 only)

Windows XP Professional Edition and Windows 2000 contain a vulnerability in one of their screensavers that could allow a criminal to hack into your system. If the Windows login screen has been on your monitor for more than ten minutes and you have not pressed any buttons on the keyboard, then a screensaver will run. The problem with this screensaver is that a criminal could use a widely known method of replacing it with a small executable file that could allow him or her to change your password and access your computer. Here is how to prevent it:

1. Click the Start button in the lower-left corner of Windows.

2. Click Run.

3. A window opens. Type **regedit** in the blank (see Figure 2-1), and then click OK or press the Enter key on your keyboard.

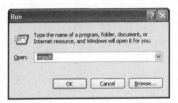

Figure 2-1

4. The Windows Registry Editor opens. Double-click the registry key HKEY_USERS. If you can't find it, do the following:

   a. In the left window pane of the Registry Editor, scroll to the top.

   b. If any of the HKEY registry keys are open—as indicated by a minus sign (–) on their left side—then close them by clicking that minus sign. When a registry key has been properly closed, it will have a plus sign (+) next to it.

   c. Repeat this process for the remaining HKEY registry keys until the only things visible in the left window pane are the five HKEY keys (see Figure 2-2).

   d. Double-click the HKEY_USERS registry key.

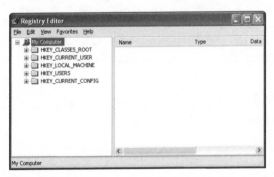

Figure 2-2

5. A new column of registry keys appears. Double-click the one labeled .Default.

6. Another column of registry keys appears. Double-click the one labeled Control Panel.

7. Click the Desktop registry key (see Figure 2-3).

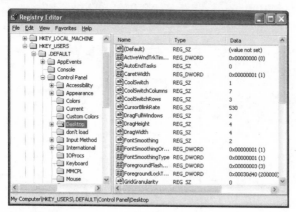

Figure 2-3

8. On the right side of the Windows Registry Editor, a list of registry values appears. Double-click SCRNSAVE.EXE (see Figure 2-4).

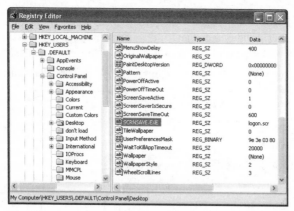

Figure 2-4

9. A window opens, inside of which is the text logon.scr. Delete it, and in its place type **none** (see Figure 2-5).

Figure 2-5

10. Click OK.

11. Double-click the registry value ScreenSaveActive (see Figure 2-6).

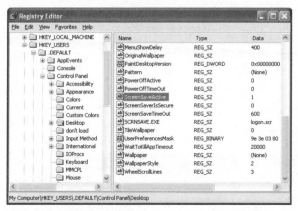

Figure 2-6

12. A window opens, inside of which is the number 1. Delete this number, and in its place type **No** (see Figure 2-7).

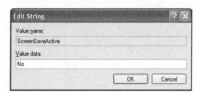

Figure 2-7

13. Click OK.

14. To exit the Registry Editor, click the X button in the upper-right corner.

Rename the Administrator Account (Windows XP Pro and Windows 2000 only)

By default, Windows XP Professional Edition and Windows 2000 contain an administrator account that has full access to all areas of your computer. Because hackers are aware of this, all they have to do to break into your computer is figure out the password for your administrator account. Give your computer enhanced protection by renaming your administrator account:

1. Click the Start button in the lower-left corner of Windows.

2. Click the Control Panel. (If you don't see this option, then your Start menu is in classic mode. In that case, click Settings, and then select the Control Panel.)

3. If the Control Panel is in category view, click the Performance and Maintenance category, and then click the Administrative Tools icon. If the Control Panel is in classic view, simply double-click the Administrative Tools icon.

4. Double-click the Computer Management icon.

5. A window opens. In the left window pane, double-click the Local Users and Groups icon.

6. Double-click the Users icon.

7. In the right window pane, right-click the Administrator account.

8. Select Rename (see Figure 2-8).

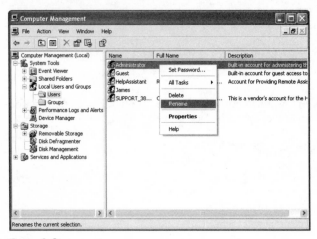

Figure 2-8

9. Type a new name for the administrative account. Your current password for the account will not be changed.

10. You can increase your security by creating a new password for the renamed administrator account. Simply right-click the account and select Set Password (see Figure 2-9).

11. Click the Proceed button.

12. Another screen appears, into which you can type a new password.

13. Click OK.

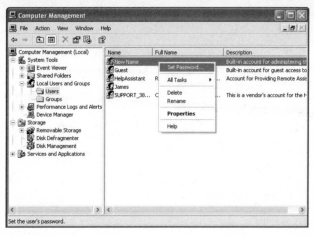

Figure 2-9

Disable the Guest Account
(Windows XP Home/Pro and Windows 2000 only)

Windows has another default account that can allow hackers to sneak into your computer if they can guess the proper password. Although the Guest account has limited access and privileges, it still has enough functionality to give hackers a field day. For this reason, you should consider disabling the Guest account.

For Windows XP Professional Edition and Windows 2000

1. Click the Start button in the lower-left corner of Windows.

2. Click the Control Panel. (If you don't see this option, then your start menu is in classic mode. In that case, click Settings, and then select the Control Panel.)

3. If the Control Panel is in category view, click the Performance and Maintenance category, and then click the Administrative Tools icon. If the Control Panel is in classic view, simply double-click the led Administrative Tools icon.

4. Double-click the Computer Management icon.

5. A window opens. In the left window pane, double-click the Local Users and Groups icon.

6. Double-click the Users icon.

7. In the right window pane, right-click the Guest account.

8. Select Properties (see Figure 2-10).

9. A window appears. Put a checkmark in the Account is Disabled box.

10. Click Apply.

11. Click OK.

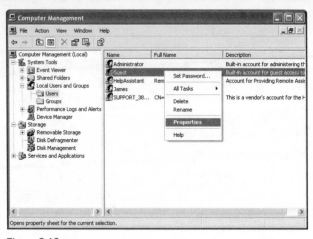

Figure 2-10

For Windows XP Home Edition

1. Click the Start button in the lower-left corner of Windows.

2. Click the Control Panel. (If you don't see this option, then your Start menu is in classic mode. In that case, click Settings, and then select the Control Panel.)

3. If the Control Panel is in category view, click the User Accounts category. If the Control Panel is in classic view, simply double-click the User Accounts icon.

4. A window opens. Click the words Change an Account.

5. Click the Guest account.

6. Click the words Turn off the Guest account (see Figure 2-11).

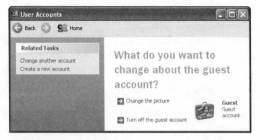

Figure 2-11

Disable Remote Desktop (Windows XP Pro only)

Windows XP Professional Edition has a feature named Remote Desktop that allows you to connect to your computer from an external location and have full access to your system. It was designed with traveling businesspersons in mind who might need to use a computer at a hotel or Internet café to dial in to their office computers and retrieve files they left behind. Despite its noble intentions, Remote Desktop poses a threat. If a hacker uncovers the right information about your Windows account, he can use it to access your computer remotely and view all of your private data—just as if he were actually sitting in front of your console.

1. Right-click the My Computer icon on your desktop. If this icon is not available, then click the Start button in the lower-left corner of Windows and right-click My Computer. If you can't find the My Computer icon anywhere, do the following:

   a. Right-click in the empty space on your desktop.

   b. Select Properties.

   c. In the window that opens, click the Desktop tab.

   d. Near the bottom of the window, click the Customize Desktop button.

   e. Another window opens. On the General tab, beneath the words Desktop Icons, place a checkmark in the My Computer box.

   f. Click OK.

   g. You are returned to the previous screen. Click the Apply button.

   h. Click OK.

   i. The My Computer icon appears on your desktop. Right-click it.

2. Select Properties.

3. Click the Remote tab.

4. Under the Remote Desktop heading, clear the checkmark from the Allow users to connect remotely to this computer box (see Figure 2-12).

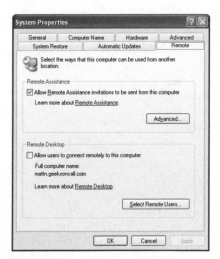

Figure 2-12

5. Click the Apply button.

6. Click OK.

Disable Remote Assistance (Windows XP Home/Pro only)

Remote Assistance is a feature in Windows XP that allows you to invite a friend, family member, or trusted person to connect to your computer via the Internet in order to troubleshoot and repair your software problems. The downside of this feature is that it could open a back door for an Internet intruder to tamper with your settings, install sinister software, or hijack your computer. Protect yourself by disabling Remote Assistance. (You can always temporarily re-enable it if you ever need it.)

1. Right-click the My Computer icon on your desktop. If this icon is not available, then click the Start button in the lower-left corner of Windows and right-click My Computer. If you can't find the My Computer icon anywhere, do the following:

   a. Right-click in the empty space on your desktop.

   b. Select Properties.

   c. In the window that opens, click the Desktop tab.

   d. Near the bottom of the window, click the Customize Desktop button.

   e. Another window opens. On the General tab, beneath the words Desktop Icons, select the My Computer box.

   f. Click OK.

   g. You are returned to the previous screen. Click Apply.

   h. Click OK.

   i. The My Computer icon appears on your desktop. Right-click it.

2. Select Properties.

3. Click the Remote tab.

4. Under the Remote Assistance heading, clear the Allow Remote Assistance invitations to be sent from this computer box (see Figure 2-13).

5. Click Apply.

6. Click OK.

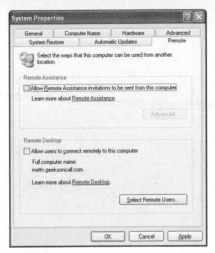

Figure 2-13

If you ever need to send a Remote Assistance invitation to someone, simply reverse these steps.

Disable File and Printer Sharing

As its name indicates, this feature enables your computer to share its files and printers over a network. If you don't operate a network in your home or office, you can make your standalone computer more safe from Internet intruders by disabling File and Printer Sharing.

For Windows XP Home Edition, XP Professional Edition, and Windows 2000

1. Click the Start button in the lower-left corner of Windows.

2. Click the Control Panel. (If you don't see this option, then your Start menu is in classic mode. In that case, click Settings, and then select the Control Panel.)

3. If the Control Panel is in category view, click the Network and Internet Connections category, and then click the Network Connections icon. If the Control Panel is in classic view, simply double-click the Network Connections icon.

4. Double-click the Local Area Connection icon.

5. On the General tab, click the Properties button.

6. A window opens. In the center of it is a list of Internet components with checkboxes next to them. Clear the File and Printer Sharing for Microsoft Networks box (see Figure 2-14).

7. Click OK.

8. Click Close.

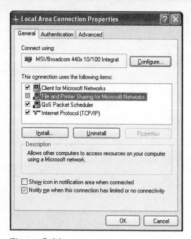

Figure 2-14

For Windows 98 and ME

1. Double-click the My Computer icon on your desktop.

2. Double-click the Control Panel icon.

3. Double-click the Network icon.

4. Click the File and Print Sharing button (see Figure 2-15).

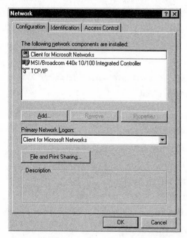

Figure 2-15

5. Clear the checkmark from the I Want to Be Able to Give Others Access to My Files box.

6. Clear the checkmark from the I Want to Be Able to Allow Others to Print to My Printers(s) box.

7. Click OK.

Clear the Pagefile (Windows XP Home/Pro and Windows 2000 only)

Also known as *virtual memory,* the Pagefile is a digital warehouse that provides your computer with extra storage space. Occasionally your passwords, usernames, or other private data can find their way into the Pagefile and remain there for quite a while. This is a security risk because if a hacker breaks into your computer, he can access the Pagefile and view your sensitive information. To prevent data from lingering in the Pagefile, you can edit the Registry to force Windows to clear this file each time your computer shuts down.

1. Click the Start button in the lower-left corner of Windows.

2. Click Run.

3. A window opens. Type **regedit** in the blank, and then click OK or press the Enter key on your keyboard.

4. The Windows Registry Editor opens. In the left window pane, double-click the registry key HKEY_LOCAL_MACHINE. If you can't find it, do the following:

    a. In the left window pane of the Registry Editor, scroll to the top.

    b. If any of the HKEY registry keys are open — as indicated by a minus sign (–) on their left side — then close them by clicking that minus sign. When a registry key has been properly closed, it has a plus sign (+) next to it.

    c. Repeat this process for the remaining HKEY registry keys until the only things visible in the left window pane are the five HKEY keys (see Figure 2-16).

    d. Double-click the HKEY_LOCAL_MACHINE registry key.

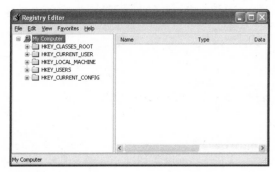

Figure 2-16

5. Beneath that, double-click the System registry key.

6. Below that, double-click the CurrentControlSet registry key.

7. Double-click the Control registry key (see Figure 2-17).

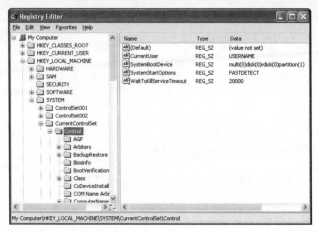

Figure 2-17

8. A long list of new registry keys appears. Scroll down the list until you see the Session Manager registry key and double-click it.

9. Click the Memory Management registry key.

10. In the right window pane, double-click ClearPageFileAtShutdown (see Figure 2-18).

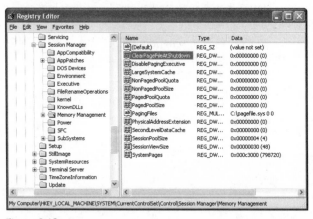

Figure 2-18

11. A box opens. The Value data text box shows a zero. Delete this number and in its place type 1 (see Figure 2-19).

12. Click OK.

13. To exit the Registry Editor, click the X button in the upper-right corner.

Figure 2-19

Disable the Dump File
(Windows XP Home/Pro and Windows 2000 only)

When Windows hits a snag, it typically sends information about the error to a storehouse known as a Dump File. This is problematic because the Dump File also keeps a record of private information — such as passwords — that would be a goldmine to an Internet intruder. You can enhance your privacy by disabling the creation of a Dump File.

Note
This process is easily reversed if you ever need to troubleshoot a Windows crash.

1. Click the Start button in the lower-left corner of Windows.

2. Click the Control Panel. (If you don't see this option, then your Start menu is in classic mode. In that case, click Settings, and then select the Control Panel.)

3. If the Control Panel is in category view, click the Performance and Maintenance category, and then click the System icon. If the Control Panel is in classic view, simply double-click the System icon.

4. A window opens. Click the Advanced tab.

5. Under the Startup and Recovery heading, click the Settings button (if you are using Windows XP) or click the Startup and Recovery button (if you are using Windows 2000).

6. Toward the bottom of the window are the words Write debugging information (see Figure 2-20). Below them is a drop-down menu. Click it and choose None.

7. Click OK.

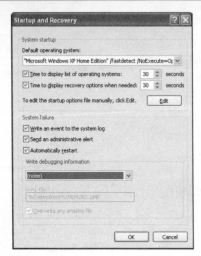

Figure 2-20

Disable Simple File Sharing (Windows XP Pro only)

Simple File Sharing is another feature of Windows that allows you to share certain folders with everyone on a network. If your computer is not part of a network, you can protect yourself from hackers by disabling this option. Even if your computer is networked, disabling Simple File Sharing can still benefit you by requiring people to know your password in order to access your shared folders.

1. Double-click the My Computer icon on your desktop. If this icon is not available, then click the Start button in the lower-left corner of Windows and click My Computer. If you can't find the My Computer icon anywhere, do the following:

    a. Right-click in the empty space on your desktop.

    b. Select Properties.

    c. A window opens. Click the Desktop tab.

    d. Near the bottom of the window, click the Customize Desktop button.

    e. Another window opens. On the General tab, beneath the words Desktop Icons, select the My Computer box.

    f. Click OK.

    g. You are returned to the previous screen. Click Apply.

    h. Click OK.

    i. The My Computer icon appears on your desktop. Right-click it.

2. Click the Tools drop-down menu.

3. Select Folder Options.

4. Click the View tab.

5. In the Advanced Settings section, scroll down until you see the words Use simple file sharing (Recommended). Next to them, remove the checkmark from the box (see Figure 2-21).

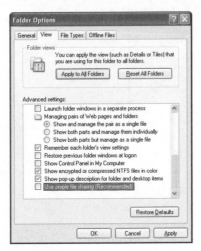

Figure 2-21

6. Click OK.

Remove Web Servers

Some versions of Windows have a built-in Web server program either called IIS (Internet Information Services) or Personal Web Server. Home users or small businesses that don't run a Web server should disable this feature to reduce attacks from digital threats.

For Windows XP Professional Edition and Windows 2000

1. Click the Start button in the lower-left corner of Windows.

2. Click the Control Panel. (If you don't see this option, then your Start menu is in classic mode. In that case, click Settings, and then select the Control Panel.)

3. If the Control Panel is in category view, click the Add or Remove Programs category. If the Control Panel is in classic view, simply double-click the Add or Remove Programs icon.

4. A window opens. In the left column, click Add/Remove Windows Components.

5. Another window opens. Scroll down the Components list until you see the words Internet Information Services (IIS). Next to them, remove the checkmark from the box (see Figure 2-22).

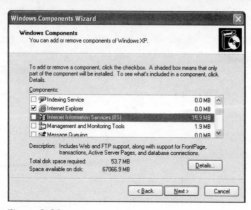

Figure 2-22

6. Click Next.

7. Click Finish.

For Windows 98 and ME

1. Double-click the My Computer icon on your desktop.

2. Double-click the Control Panel.

3. Double-click the Add/Remove Programs icon.

4. Click the Windows Setup tab.

5. Scroll down and single-click the words Internet Tools.

6. Click the Details button.

7. Clear the Personal Web Server checkbox (see Figure 2-23).

Figure 2-23

8. Click OK.

9. Click Apply.

10. Click OK again.

Modify the Hosts File

Another method of blocking unwanted Internet advertisements and hazardous Web sites is to modify a Windows file named hosts. There are two ways to do this.

Automatically

Many popular anti-spyware programs such as Spy Sweeper or Spybot Search and Destroy can automatically modify, manage, and protect your hosts file and keep it updated with new lists of advertisements or Web sites to block.

Manually

Regardless of whether or not you use an anti-spyware program to modify the hosts file, you also have the option to manually edit it.

Note

All changes made to the hosts file are permanent unless you undo them by reversing these instructions.

For XP Home Edition, XP Professional Edition, and Windows 2000

1. Double-click the My Computer icon on your desktop. If this icon is not available, then click the Start menu in the lower-left corner of Windows and click My Computer. If you can't find the My Computer icon anywhere, do the following:

    a. Right-click in the empty space on your desktop.

    b. Select Properties.

    c. A window opens. Click the Desktop tab.

    d. Near the bottom of the window, click the Customize Desktop button.

    e. Another window opens. On the General tab, beneath the words Desktop Icons, select the My Computer checkbox.

    f. Click OK.

    g. You are returned to the previous screen. Click Apply.

    h. Click OK.

    i. The My Computer icon appears on your desktop. Right-click it.

2. Double-click the C: drive (unless you installed Windows in a different location, in which case you would double-click that drive letter).

3. If you are using Windows XP, double-click the Windows folder. If you are using Windows 2000, double-click the WINNT folder.

4. If you see a message that says "This Folder Contains Files That Keep Your System Working Properly. There Is No Need to Modify Its Contents," then click the words below it that say Show Files.

5. Double-click the System 32 folder.

6. Double-click the Drivers folder.

7. Double-click the Etc folder.

8. Look for a file named hosts. If only one file has this name, then proceed to Step 9. If you see more than one file named hosts, then do the following:

   a. Right-click the first hosts file.

   b. Select Properties.

   c. A window opens. Click the General tab.

   d. Next to the Type of File heading, it should say File. Next to the Description heading, it should say hosts. If you can see this information, then you have selected the proper hosts file.

   e. Click OK.

9. Right-click the hosts file.

10. Select Open.

11. A window opens asking you to "Choose the program you want to use to open this file." Scroll down and double-click Notepad (see Figure 2-24).

Figure 2-24

12. The Notepad program opens and displays the contents of your hosts file. At the top, the first line of text should say 127.0.0.1 local host. Beneath this, use your keyboard to create a new line of text that starts with 127.0.0.1 followed by a space and then the name of the Web site you want to block (see Figure 2-25). For example, type 127.0.0.1 www.badsite.com to block a fictitious site named www.badsite.com.

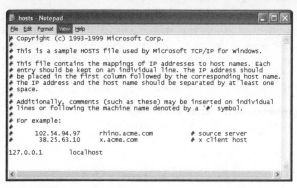

Figure 2-25

13. When you have finished modifying your hosts file, click the File drop-down menu in the upper-left corner of Notepad.

14. Select Save.

15. To exit Notepad, click the X button in the upper-right corner.

For Windows 98 and ME

1. Double-click the My Computer icon on your desktop.

2. Double-click the C: drive (unless you installed Windows in a different location, in which case you would double-click that drive letter).

3. Double-click the Windows folder.

4. If you see a message that says This Folder Contains Files That Keep Your System Working Properly. There Is No Need to Modify Its Contents, then click the words below it that say Show Files.

5. Look for a file named hosts. If only one file has this name, then proceed to Step 6. If you see more than one file named hosts, then do the following:

    a. Right-click the first hosts file.

    b. Select Properties.

    c. A window opens. Click the General tab.

    d. Next to the Type of File heading, it should say File. Next to the Description heading, it should say hosts. If you can see this information, then you have selected the proper hosts file.

    e. Click OK.

6. Right-click the hosts file.

7. Select Open With.

8. From the list, select Notepad.

9. The Notepad program opens and displays the contents of your hosts file. At the top, the first line of text should say 127.0.0.1 local host. Beneath this, use your keyboard to create a new line of text that starts with 127.0.0.1 followed by a space and then the name of the Web site you want to block. For example, you would type 127.0.0.1 www.badsite.com to block a site named www.badsite.com.

10. When you have finished modifying your hosts file, click the File drop-down menu in the upper-left corner of Notepad.

11. Select Save.

12. To exit Notepad, click the X button in the upper-right corner.

Unhide File Extensions

Windows automatically hides the extensions for common, everyday files. Knowing this, many viruses hide inside files that end with two different extensions—a safe one followed by a dangerous one (such as File.txt.vbs). Because computer users can see only the first extension, they assume the file is safe and open it—which launches the virus. To discover the true extensions of the files on your computer, you must tell Windows to reveal all file extensions at all times.

For Windows XP Home Edition, XP Professional Edition, and Windows 2000

1. Click the Start button located in the lower-left corner of Windows.

2. Click the Control Panel. (If you don't see this option, then your Start menu is in classic mode. In that case, click Settings, and then select the Control Panel.)

3. If the Control Panel is in category view, click the Appearance and Themes category, and then click the Folder Options icon. If the Control Panel is in classic view, simply double-click the Folder Options icon.

4. A window opens. Click the View tab.

5. You will see a list of options and a scroll bar. Scroll down until you see the Hide extensions for known file types checkbox and clear the checkmark (see Figure 2-26).

6. Click Apply.

7. Click OK.

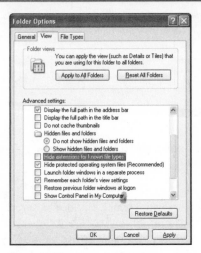

Figure 2-26

For Windows 98 and ME

1. Double-click the My Computer icon on your desktop.

2. Click the View drop-down menu.

3. Select Folder Options.

4. Click the View tab.

5. Clear the Hide File Extensions for Known File Types checkbox.

6. Click Apply.

7. Click OK.

Unhide Special Extensions

Even if you have followed the steps to make common file extensions visible, there are some extensions that Windows still keeps hidden, such as .pif, .shs, .lnk, and "CLIDs." Often these files are used by criminals to spread viruses or similar digital threats. To decrease your chances of being tricked into opening an infected e-mail attachment, you can force Windows to reveal these special file extensions. To do so, you will need to edit the Windows Registry.

1. Click the Start button in the lower-left corner of Windows.

2. Select Run.

3. A window opens. Type **regedit** in the blank, and then click OK or press the Enter key on your keyboard.

4. The Windows Registry Editor opens. Click the Edit drop-down menu in the upper-left corner.

5. Select Find.

6. A window opens. Next to the words Find What, type **NeverShowExt** (see Figure 2-27).

Figure 2-27

7. Double-check your spelling of NeverShowExt to make certain it looks *exactly* as it appears in Figure 2-27.

8. Click the Find Next button.

9. The Registry Editor searches your registry, which could take several minutes depending on the speed of your computer. When the search is complete, you will see an entry named NeverShowExt in the right window pane of the Registry Editor.

10. Click NeverShowExt and then press the Delete key on your keyboard, or right-click this entry and select Delete (see Figure 2-28).

Figure 2-28

11. Press the F3 key on your keyboard, which begins a search for the next registry entry named NeverShowExt.

12. When the search is done, delete the next occurrence of NeverShowExt.

13. Use the F3 key to search as many times as necessary until all registry entries named NeverShowExt have been deleted.

14. When you're finished, exit the Registry Editor by clicking the X button in the upper-right corner.

Disable VBScripts

Visual Basic Scripts (*VBScripts* for short) are text files containing programming code that have the file extension .vbs. Often criminals hide viruses or similar digital threats inside VBScripts and attach them to e-mail. When you open the attachment, the VBScript code is launched and the virus infects your computer.

To give your system maximum protection, you should consider disabling VBScripts.

For Windows XP Home Edition, XP Professional Edition, and Windows 2000

1. Double-click the My Computer icon on your desktop. If this icon is not available, then click the Start button in the lower-left corner of Windows and click My Computer. If you can't find the My Computer icon anywhere, do the following:

   a. Right-click in the empty space on your desktop.

   b. Select Properties.

   c. A window opens. Click the Desktop tab.

   d. Near the bottom of the window, click the Customize Desktop button.

   e. Another window opens. On the General tab, beneath the words Desktop Icons, select the My Computer checkbox.

   f. Click OK.

   g. You are returned to the previous screen. Click Apply.

   h. Click OK.

   i. The My Computer icon appears on your desktop. Right-click it.

2. Click the Tools drop-down menu.

3. Select Folder Options.

4. Click the File Types tab.

5. In the Registered file types section, scroll down to find the VBS extension with the file type VBScript Script File (see Figure 2-29).

Figure 2-29

6. On the right side of the window, click the Delete button.

7. If a message asks Are You Sure You Want to Remove This Extension, click Yes.

Repeat these steps for the following file types:

- JScript Script File (with the extension JS)
- JScript Encoded Script File (with the extension JSE)
- VBScript Encoded Script File (with the extension VBE)
- Windows Script File (with the extension WSF)

For Windows 98 and ME

1. Click the Start button in the lower-left corner of Windows.

2. Click Settings.

3. Select the Control Panel.

4. Double-click the Add/Remove Programs icon.

5. Click the Windows Setup tab.

6. In the center of the window, click Accessories.

7. Toward the bottom of the window, click the Details button.

8. Another window opens. Scroll down the list until you see the Windows Scripting Host checkbox. Clear the checkmark.

9. Click OK.

10. You are returned to the Add/Remove Programs window. Click Apply.

11. Click OK.

Alternate Method for Windows XP Home Edition, XP Professional Edition, and Windows 2000

If you want to retain the ability to run VBScripts at some point in the future, then don't remove them completely. Here is an alternate tweak that allows them to stay but prevents them from launching automatically.

1. Double-click the My Computer icon on your desktop. If this icon is not available, then click the Start button in the lower-left corner of Windows and click My Computer. If you can't find the My Computer icon anywhere, do the following:

   a. Right-click in the empty space on your desktop.

   b. Select Properties.

   c. A window opens. Click the Desktop tab.

   d. Near the bottom of the window, click the Customize Desktop button.

e. Another window opens. On the General tab, beneath the words Desktop Icons, place a checkmark in the My Computer box.

f. Click OK.

g. You are returned to the previous screen. Click Apply.

h. Click OK.

i. The My Computer icon appears on your desktop. Right-click it.

2. Click the Tools drop-down menu.

3. Select Folder Options.

4. Click the File Types tab.

5. Under the subheading also labeled File Types, scroll down until you find the words VBScript Script File. Their extension is VBS.

6. Click the Advanced button.

7. A window opens. Under the Actions heading are the options Edit, Open, Print, and Open with Command Prompt. Click Edit to highlight it, but don't double-click it.

8. On the right side of the window are four buttons: New, Edit, Remove, and Set Default. Click Set Default.

9. Select the Confirm open after download checkbox, and then select the Always show extension checkbox.

10. Click OK.

Repeat these steps for the following file types:

- JScript Script File (with the extension JS)

- JScript Encoded Script File (with the extension JSE)

- VBScript Encoded Script File (with the extension VBE)

- Windows Script File (with the extension WSF)

11. When finished, close the Folder Options window by clicking Close button.

Disable Messenger (Windows XP Home/Pro and Windows 2000)

Windows has a feature known as Messenger that was designed as an easy way for administrators of a computer network to send messages to each computer that is plugged into the network. Unfortunately, this same feature opens a hole that allows Internet worms and pop-up advertisements to invade your system. If you have Windows 2000 or if you have Windows XP but have not downloaded the Service Pack 2 security update, then the Messenger problem exists on your computer and must be disabled.

Note
Don't confuse this Messenger service with the instant-message program built into Windows XP called Windows Messenger—the two are completely different.

Warning
If your computer does not have the most recent Windows security patches installed, then wait to retrieve them from the Internet until after you have followed these steps to disable the Messenger service.

1. Disconnect from the Internet to prevent worms or digital threats from slipping into your computer before you can disable Messenger.

2. Click the Start button in the lower-left corner of Windows.

3. Click the Control Panel. (If you don't see this option, then your Start menu is in classic mode. In that case, click Settings, and then select the Control Panel.)

4. If the Control Panel is in category view, click Performance and Maintenance category, and then click the Administrative Tools icon. If the Control Panel is in classic view, simply double-click the Administrative Tools icon.

5. Double-click the Services icon.

6. A window opens. Using the scroll bar, scroll down until you see the word Messenger and double-click it (see Figure 2-30).

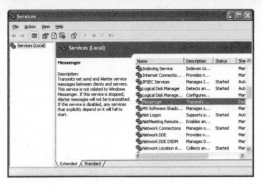

Figure 2-30

7. Another window opens. In the middle of it, look for the words Startup
Type. Next to them, click the drop-down menu and select Disabled
(see Figure 2-31).

Figure 2-31

8. Click the Apply button.

9. Click OK.

PART II

E-MAIL SECURITY

Give E-Mail a Whole New Outlook

Because Microsoft's e-mail programs, Outlook (which comes with Microsoft Office) and Outlook Express (which comes free with Windows), are so popular and widely used, they are primary targets for criminals who want to spread chaos through viruses and worms. If you use either of these programs to send or receive e-mail, you must take action to protect yourself from digital threats.

3

PROTECT OUTLOOK EXPRESS

By default, Outlook Express does not turn on all possible security features (unless you have Service Pack 2 installed on Windows XP, in which case most — if not all — of these settings are automatically enabled). To determine if you have Service Pack 2, do the following:

1. Click the Start button in the lower-left corner of Windows.

2. Click the Control Panel. (If you don't see this option, then your Start menu is in classic mode. In that case, click Settings, and then select the Control Panel.)

3. If the Control Panel is in category view, click the Performance and Maintenance category, and then click the System icon. If the Control Panel is in classic view, simply double-click the System icon.

4. A window opens. On the General tab, look for the word System. Beneath it, you should see some words identifying your version of Windows XP as well as any service packs that have been installed.

Do It Yourself

Enable maximum security

Disable the Preview pane

Safely view e-mail

Read e-mail in plain text (Outlook Express 6 only)

Send e-mail in plain text

View a blocked e-mail attachment

Enable Maximum Security

To provide Outlook Express with the highest level of protection, turn on its maximum-security settings.

Note

Using maximum security may reduce the functionality of some features in Outlook Express, but it is a small price to pay for enhanced security.

1. Open Outlook Express

2. Click the Tools drop-down menu.

3. Select Options.

4. Click the Security tab.

5. Under the words Virus Protection, select Restricted Sites Zone (More Secure).

6. Put a checkmark in the Warn me when other applications try to send mail as me box.

7. Put a checkmark in the box Do not allow attachments to be saved or opened that could potentially be a virus (see Figure 3-1).

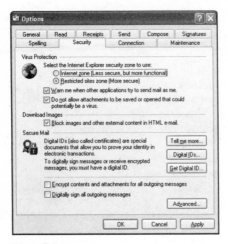

Figure 3-1

8. Put a checkmark in the Block images and other external content in HTML e-mail box.

9. Click Apply.

10. Click the Maintenance tab.

11. Put a checkmark in the Purge deleted messages when leaving IMAP folders box.

12. Click Apply.

13. Click OK.

Disable the Preview Pane

Outlook Express has a feature known as the Preview pane that creates a split screen: One half shows all of your e-mail, and the second half shows the content of the message that is currently selected. The purpose of this feature is to let you view an e-mail simply by selecting it from the list rather than double-clicking it. Despite the convenience, using the Preview pane is the same thing as opening an e-mail; lewd images can appear, e-mail can be decoded, dangerous programming scripts can run, viruses can launch, and spammers may be alerted that you have opened their e-mail. To protect your privacy, disable the Preview pane.

1. Open Outlook Express.

2. In the left window pane, click the Inbox folder. If you don't see a vertical list of folders, then do the following:

   a. Click the View drop-down menu.

   b. Select Layout.

   c. Under the Basic heading, put a checkmark in the Folder List box.

   d. Click Apply.

   e. Click OK.

   f. Click the Inbox folder.

3. Click the View drop-down menu.

4. Select Layout.

5. Remove the checkmark from the Show preview pane box (see Figure 3-2).

Figure 3-2

6. Click Apply.

7. Click OK.

8. Repeat this procedure for all additional Outlook Express folders in which you view or store e-mail.

Safely View E-Mail

Outlook Express enables you to view the details of an e-mail without opening the actual message. Use this *passive viewer* to help you decide whether or not an e-mail is safe to open.

1. In your e-mail Inbox or e-mail folder, right-click the e-mail in question.

2. Choose Properties.

3. Click the Details tab.

4. Select Message Source.

5. A window opens. This is the passive viewer. Scroll down until you see some words displayed in a bold font. This is the subject line or header of the e-mail. The words displayed in a regular font are the main text or body of the e-mail.

6. When you are finished using the passive viewer, close it. If you decide the e-mail is safe, then open it normally. If you decide the e-mail is unsafe, then right-click it and select Delete.

Read E-Mail in Plain Text (Outlook Express 6 only)

Some e-mail messages are created in HTML format, which allows their text to be enhanced by images and other graphical content. The problem with these messages is that viruses or other digital threats can hide inside the HTML code and spring to life when you open the e-mail. To prevent this, you can force Outlook Express to display all of your e-mail in harmless, plain text.

1. Open Outlook Express.

2. Click the Tools drop-down menu.

3. Select Options.

4. Select Read.

5. Put a checkmark in the Read all messages in plain text box (see Figure 3-3).

Figure 3-3

6. Click Apply.

7. Click OK.

Send E-Mail in Plain Text

To give your friends, family, and acquaintances peace of mind about the safety of the e-mail you send them, consider writing in the plain-text format.

1. Open Outlook Express.

2. Click the Tools drop-down menu.

3. Select Options.

4. Click the Send tab.

5. Under the Mail Sending Format heading, select Plain Text (see Figure 3-4).

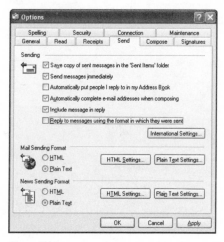

Figure 3-4

6. Under the News Sending Format heading, select Plain Text.

7. Click Apply.

8. Click OK.

View a Blocked E-Mail Attachment

If you use the maximum security settings for Outlook Express, you will discover that it automatically blocks some attachments you may want to receive. This applies only to attachments such as executable programs that are widely regarded as carriers of viruses or other digital threats. If you want to receive a blocked attachment, you can temporarily disable this feature.

1. Open Outlook Express.

2. Click the Tools drop-down menu.

3. Select Options.

4. Click the Security tab.

5. Remove the checkmark from the Do not allow attachments to be saved or opened that could potentially be a virus box.

6. Click Apply.

7. Click OK.

8. When you have finished viewing or opening the attachment, return to the Security tab and put back the checkmark in the Do not allow attachments to be saved or opened that could potentially be a virus box.

9. Click Apply.

10. Click OK.

4

PROTECT OUTLOOK

5-Minute Fixes

Microsoft's Outlook is a multifaceted program that can be used to manage e-mail, keep track of appointments, create to-do lists, and much more. However, it too must be tweaked to provide maximum protection from digital threats.

Download the Latest Security Patches and Service Packs for Microsoft Office

Microsoft Office programs such as Outlook must be updated with the most recent security patches to protect them — and you — from digital threats and Internet criminals. No matter how old or new your Office programs are, you should visit the Office Update Web site every few months to see if new patches have been released. For more information on how to update Outlook and all your Office programs, refer to Chapter 1.

Disable the Preview Pane

Outlook has a feature known as the Preview pane that creates a split screen: One half shows all of your e-mail, and the second half shows the content of the message that is currently selected. The purpose of this feature is to let you view an e-mail simply by selecting it from the list rather than double-clicking it. Despite the convenience, using the Preview pane is the same thing as opening an e-mail; lewd images can appear, e-mail can be decoded, dangerous programming scripts can run, viruses can launch, and spammers may be alerted that you have opened their e-mail. To protect your privacy, disable the Preview Pane.

For Outlook 2000 and Outlook XP
1. Open Outlook.
2. Click the View drop-down menu.
3. Click Preview Pane. This disables it.

Do It Yourself

Download the latest security patches and service packs for Microsoft Office

Disable the Preview pane

Safely view e-mail details

Read e-mail in plain text

Send e-mail in plain text

Turn on attachment alerts

4. Repeat these steps for each Outlook folder in which you view or store e-mail.

For Outlook 2003

1. Open Outlook.

2. Click the View drop-down menu.

3. Click Reading Pane.

4. Select Off.

5. Repeat these steps for each Outlook folder in which you view or store e-mail.

Safely View E-Mail Details

Although Outlook does not have a passive viewer similar to Outlook Express, you can view a few details about an e-mail without opening it. This will assist you in determining whether or not an e-mail is potentially risky or carries a dangerous attachment.

1. Open Outlook.

2. Make sure the Preview pane is disabled.

3. Right-click the e-mail in question.

4. Select Options.

5. A Message Options window opens. Toward the bottom of this window, look for the words Internet Headers. Next to them are details about your e-mail.

6. Using the scroll bar on the right, scroll through the details until you see the word From on the left side of the window. Next to it is the e-mail address from which the message was sent.

7. If there is a file attached to the e-mail, you can view details about it by scrolling down to the words Content-Type. This tells you what type of file is attached. Beneath these words it should say Name =. This tells you the full name of the attached file (including its extension). If the file is a type known to carry digital threats, or if the file has two extensions, then you know not to open it.

Read E-Mail in Plain Text

Some e-mail messages are created in HTML format, which allows their text to be enhanced by images and other graphical content. The problem with these messages is that viruses or other digital threats can hide inside the HTML code and spring to life when you open the e-mail. To prevent this, you can force Outlook to display all of your e-mail in harmless, plain text.

For Outlook 2000

This older version of Outlook cannot view e-mail in plain text because it is auto-matically configured to reply to an e-mail in the same format as the original message. For this reason, it is recommended that you upgrade to a newer version of Outlook.

For Outlook XP (with Service Pack 1)

To enable Outlook to read non–digitally signed e-mail or non-encrypted e-mail in plain text, you will have to edit the Windows Registry.

1. Click the Start menu in the lower-left corner of Windows.

2. Click Run.

3. A window opens. Type **regedit** in the blank, and then click OK or press the Enter key on your keyboard.

4. The Windows Registry Editor opens. In the left window pane, double-click the registry key HKEY_CURRENT_USER. If you can't find it, do the following:

   a. In the left window pane of the Registry Editor, scroll to the top.

   b. If any of the HKEY registry keys are open — as indicated by a minus sign (–) on their left side — then close them by clicking that minus sign. When a registry key has been properly closed, it will have a plus sign (+) next to it.

   c. Repeat this process for the remaining HKEY registry keys until the only things visible in the left window pane are the five HKEY keys (see Figure 4-1).

   d. Double-click the HKEY_CURRENT_USER registry key.

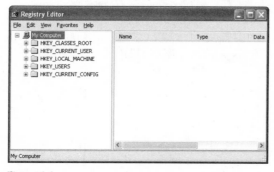

Figure 4-1

5. Beneath it, double-click the Software registry key.

6. Below it, double-click the Microsoft registry key.

7. Double-click the Office registry key.

8. Double-click the 10.0 registry key.

9. Double-click the Outlook registry key.

10. Double-click the Options registry key.

11. Double-click the Mail registry key.

12. In the upper-left corner of the Registry Editor, click the Edit drop-down menu.

13. Select New.

14. Select DWORD Value (see Figure 4-2).

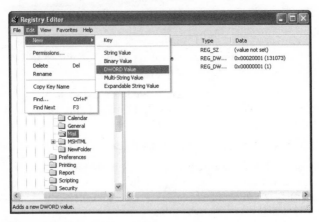

Figure 4-2

15. In the right window pane, a new registry value appears. Rename it ReadAsPlain (see Figure 4-3).

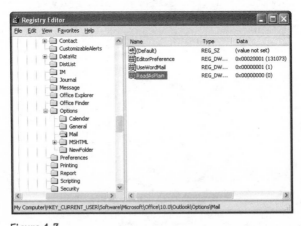

Figure 4-3

16. After renaming the value, double-click it to open it.

17. Under the Value data heading, type **1** (see Figure 4-4).

Figure 4-4

18. Click OK.

19. To exit the Registry Editor, click the "X" button in the upper-right corner.

For Outlook 2003

1. Open Outlook.

2. Click the Tools drop-down menu.

3. Select Options.

4. Click the Preferences tab.

5. Click the E-Mail Options button.

6. Put a checkmark in the Read all standard mail in plain text box.

7. Beneath it, put a checkmark in the Read all digitally signed mail in plain text box.

8. Click OK.

Send E-Mail in Plain Text

You can configure Outlook to create and send e-mail in the plain-text format, which gives the recipients of your messages peace of mind about the safety of your e-mail.

For Outlook 2000, Outlook XP, and Outlook 2003

1. Open Outlook.

2. Click the Tools drop-down menu.

3. Select Options.

4. Click the Mail Format tab.

5. In Outlook 2000, look for the words Send in This Message Format. In Outlook XP and Outlook 2003, look for the words Compose in This Message Format.

6. Use the drop-down menu to select Plain Text.

7. Click Apply.

8. Click OK.

Turn on Attachment Alerts

Outlook enables you to turn on a visual alert that will appear each time you try to open an e-mail attachment that is potentially dangerous.

Note

You can turn this alert on or off only in the versions of Outlook prior to 2002. Beginning with Outlook 2002, these alerts are automatic.

1. Open Outlook.

2. Click the Tools drop-down menu.

3. Select Options.

4. Click the Attachment Security button.

5. A window opens. Click the High (Recommended for All Users) option.

6. Click OK.

PART III

DIGITAL THREATS

It's Not Paranoia If They're Really Out to Get You

A few minutes. That's how long you can use the Internet before your unprotected computer is infected with a virus, worm, or spyware. Who creates these digital threats? Why do they want to harm you? No one knows for sure. But one thing is certain: The only way to stay safe is to install special software, tweak Windows, and establish good habits.

5

VIRUSES AND WORMS

A virus is a small program that is injected into your computer when you open or run an infected file.

Symptoms of Virus or Worm Infection

Most computers that are infected with a virus or worm exhibit common symptoms. Think of them as the high-tech version of a runny nose or a fever.

Crash! This could take many forms: "fatal error" messages (often referred to as the "Blue Screen of Death"); "illegal operation" messages; the computer shutting down unexpectedly; or being unable to start Windows.

Freeze! Your computer suddenly enters a state of suspended animation in which everything onscreen freezes (or perhaps you can move your mouse around the screen but you are unable to click on anything).

Soooo slow! Your computer is slower than normal. Windows takes longer to start up or shut down. Your programs take longer to load or use. Your mouse cursor has a delayed response when you move it. When surfing the Internet, Web sites take much longer to load. Your digital music or video files do not play normally. When using a word-processing program, the words you type do not appear immediately onscreen (there is noticeable lag). Or it takes an unusual amount of time to open a folder or a window.

If your computer isn't experiencing these symptoms, don't assume it is safe. It could be infected with a stealthy worm or Trojan horse that operates silently behind the scenes, gathering data from your system and transmitting it to criminals via the Internet.

Do It Yourself

How do viruses infect a computer?

Protect your computer from viruses

Antivirus software

What damage can a virus do?

When to update your antivirus software

Protect your computer from macro viruses

How to tell if a file is infected

If you think your computer is infected with a virus

How do worms infect a computer?

What damage can a worm do?

Prevent worms from invading your computer

Disable the Preview pane in Outlook and Outlook Express

If you think your computer is infected with a worm

How Do Viruses Infect a Computer?

Generally, viruses hide inside the following:

- E-mail attachments
- Files you download from seedy Web sites or from file-sharing pro-grams used to trade pirated songs or videos
- The code of a Web page
- The text of an e-mail

Protect Your Computer from Viruses

- Install trusted, respected antivirus software and keep it updated con-stantly.
- Do not open e-mail attachments that have a file extension of .exe, .scr, or .vbs, or a double file extension such as .txt.vbs (see Figure 5-1).

File.txt.vbs

Figure 5-1

- Be wary of opening any e-mail attachments or instant-message attachments sent from people you don't know — even if those attach-ments do not have a dangerous file extension.
- Do not open spam e-mail (selling products; offering free videos, pictures, or songs; and so on).
- Perform a virus scan on files before downloading them or opening them.
- Perform a virus scan on e-mail attachments you think are safe to open.
- Do not install pirated software because often it contains viruses.
- Do not download pirated music files or videos because they too contain viruses.
- Do not click links sent to you in an instant message.

Antivirus Software

Here are some popular and trusted antivirus programs (in no particular order):

- Norton Antivirus (www.symantec.com)
- McAfee Virus Scan (www.mcafee.com)
- eTrust EZ Antivirus (www.ca.com)
- PC–cillin (www.trendmicro.com)

- AVG Anti-Virus (www.grisoft.com)

What Damage Can a Virus Do?

- Crash a computer

- Prevent the computer from booting up

- Cause Windows to become slow and sluggish

- Delete your private data

- Delete critical system files from Windows

FYI

You don't have to buy the newest version of your antivirus program each year. Instead, you can simply re-subscribe to its antivirus updates service (typically a subscription lasts for one year). That way, you only have to buy a new version of the program every few years, which will save you money.

When to Update Your Antivirus Software

No matter what antivirus program you use, it must be updated regularly to protect your computer from the newest viruses. The easiest solution is to turn on the program's automatic update feature, which will automatically download and install new antivirus updates (often called "definitions") every few days. For enhanced security, you can manually download these updates each day (if applicable).

Protect Your Computer from Macro Viruses

Some programs used for word processing or spreadsheets allow the use of a *macro*, a type of executable computer code that automates certain tasks. Although macros can be useful, they also can be exploited by criminals who want to insert a macro virus into a document. For that reason, you should increase the macro security settings in your software or consider disabling macros altogether.

1. Open your Microsoft Office program (such as Word, Excel, Access, or PowerPoint).

2. Click the Tools drop-down menu.

3. Select Macro.

4. Select Security.

5. You are presented with the option to select your macro security level. If you use Office 2000 or Office XP, choose High (see Figure 5-2). If you use Office 2003, choose Very High.

Figure 5-2

6. Click OK.

How to Tell If a File Is Infected

Most antivirus programs automatically scan files you download or open. Generally, antivirus software runs silently in the background while you use your computer and continually monitors your system. As an extra measure of security, you can manually scan a file for viruses before opening or running it. Here's how:

1. Open your antivirus program.

2. Choose the option for a *manual scan* (by telling it to scan a particular file).

Or:

1. Right-click the file in question.

2. Choose the option to Scan with [*the name of your antivirus program*]. For example, if you use Norton Antivirus, you right-click the file and select Scan with Norton Antivirus.

If You Think Your Computer Is Infected with a Virus

If your computer is experiencing symptoms of infection, you must take immediate action.

If You Have Antivirus Software Installed

1. Immediately disconnect from the Internet.

- If you use a software firewall, this can be done by turning on your Internet lock to halt all data from entering or exiting your computer.

- If you don't have a software firewall, then you must physically disconnect your Internet connection.

- If you use a dial-up Internet service such as AOL, Earthlink, or MSN, reach behind your computer and unplug the phone cord from your modem. This will prevent sneaky automatic-dialer programs from connecting to the Internet without your permission.

- If you use high-speed Internet (DSL or cable), unplug the power cable to your modem or reach behind your computer and unplug the Ethernet cable from your network interface card (NIC).

2. Launch your antivirus program and tell it to scan your entire computer for viruses. This could take quite a while (possibly an hour or more) depending on how old or slow your computer is and how much data you have.

3. If the antivirus scan finds nothing, it is possible that your software is not updated with the most recent antivirus definitions. To update your definitions, do the following:

   a. Hook up your Internet modems and cables.

   b. Connect to the Internet.

   c. Open your antivirus software and tell it to search for new updates. This method will vary depending on the particular antivirus program you use. Follow your program's onscreen instructions.

   d. Once all necessary updates have been downloaded, disconnect from the Internet just like you did when you began this process.

   e. Scan your entire computer for viruses a second time.

4. If the scan finds a virus, follow your antivirus program's onscreen instructions to remove it. Then, do the following:

   a. Hook up your Internet modems and cables.

   b. Connect to the Internet.

   c. Open your antivirus software and tell it to search for new updates. This method will vary depending upon the particular antivirus program you use. Follow your program's onscreen instructions.

   d. Once all necessary updates have been downloaded, disconnect from the Internet as you did when you began this process.

   e. Scan your entire computer for viruses a second time.

5. If you follow all of these steps and your computer still acts strangely, it might be infected with a different digital threat such as spyware. Consider installing anti-spyware software. For more information on spyware, see Chapter 6.

6. If your computer still has problems, call Geeks On Call.

Is a Worm Similar to a Virus?

No. Viruses hide inside another program or file, whereas worms are self-contained programs that can infect a computer all by themselves. Generally you have to take action to become infected with a virus (such as opening an e-mail attachment), but to be infected with a worm all you have to do is surf the Internet with a computer that lacks the latest Windows security patches.

If You Don't Have Antivirus Software Installed

The only way to remove harmful viruses from your computer is to use a trusted, respected antivirus program. If your computer doesn't have antivirus software, then you must do one of the following.

- Purchase antivirus software from a retail store, install it, and then use it to remove the virus.

- Purchase and download antivirus software from an e-merchant's Web site, install it, and then use it to remove the virus.

- Call Geeks On Call to remove the virus and install antivirus software on your computer.

It's a Fact
Each month, approximately 1,000 new computer viruses are discovered.

How Do Worms Infect a Computer?

- They hide inside e-mail attachments.

- They are automatically downloaded to your computer when you click a link in an e-mail or instant message.

- They slither through holes or flaws in Windows.

What Damage Can a Worm Do?

- Open a back door into your computer that allows it to be controlled by a criminal (this is known as turning your computer into a "zombie")

- Allow a criminal to use your computer to send spam or download illegal materials onto your hard drive (such as child pornography)

- Allow a criminal to use your computer to attack Web sites and temporarily knock them off the Internet

- Install a "keystroke logging" program that allows a criminal to see everything you type on your keyboard (including passwords and credit card numbers)

- Send copies of itself to all of the e-mail addresses listed in your address book or stored in your computer

- Slow down the Internet, making it difficult to do common tasks such as sending e-mail, doing online banking, and shopping at e-merchants

Prevent Worms from Invading Your Computer

- Most antivirus programs also scan for worms, so install a trusted, respected brand of antivirus software and keep it updated constantly.

- Download the most recent Windows patches, updates, and service packs.

- Turn on the Automatic Update feature of Windows to ensure that it automatically downloads and installs the latest Windows security fixes as soon as they are available.

- Do not open e-mail attachments that have file extensions such as .exe, .scr, and .vbs or have double file extensions such as .txt.vbs (see Figure 5-3).

Figure 5-3

- Be wary of opening e-mail attachments sent from people you don't know.

- Do not click links inside strange e-mails or in instant messages (even if the messages are sent from friends or family).

- Do not install pirated software.

- Install the most recent security updates and service packs for all Microsoft Office software (Word, Excel, Access, PowerPoint, Publisher, and so on).

Disable the Preview Pane in Outlook and Outlook Express

Outlook and Outlook Express have a feature known as the Preview pane that creates a split screen: One half shows all of your e-mail, and the other half shows the content of the message that is currently selected. The purpose of this feature is to let you view an e-mail simply by selecting it from the list rather than double-clicking it. Despite the convenience, using the Preview pane is the same thing as opening an e-mail; lewd images can appear, e-mail can be decoded, dangerous programming scripts can run, viruses can launch, and spammers can be alerted that you have opened their e-mail. To protect your privacy, disable the Preview pane.

For Outlook Express

1. Open Outlook Express.

2. In the left window pane, click the Inbox folder. If you don't see a vertical list of folders, then do the following:

   a. Click the View drop-down menu.

   b. Select Layout.

   c. Under the heading labeled Basic, put a checkmark in the Folder List box.

   d. Click Apply.

   e. Click OK.

   f. Click the Inbox folder.

3. Click the View drop-down menu.

4. Select Layout.

5. Remove the checkmark from Show preview pane checkbox.

6. Click Apply.

7. Click OK.

8. Repeat this procedure for all additional Outlook Express folders in which you view or store e-mail.

For Outlook 2000 and Outlook XP

1. Open Outlook.

2. Click the View drop-down menu.

3. Click Preview Pane. This disables it.

4. Repeat these steps for each Outlook folder in which you view or store e-mail.

For Outlook 2003

1. Open Outlook.

2. Click the View drop-down menu.

3. Click Reading Pane.

4. Select Off.

5. Repeat these steps for each Outlook folder in which you view or store e-mail.

If You Think Your Computer Is Infected with a Worm

Most computer worms can be detected and removed by antivirus software, so follow the steps listed under "If You Think Your Computer Is Infected with a Virus" earlier in this chapter.

6

SPYWARE

S pyware is a general term describing dangerous programs that sneak into your computer by tricking you into installing them or by hiding in other programs you install.

Symptoms of Spyware Infection

Most computers that are infected with spyware exhibit common symptoms. Think of them as the high-tech version of a runny nose or a fever.

> **Soooo slow:** Your computer is slower than normal. Windows takes longer to start up or shut down. Your programs take longer to load or use. Your mouse cursor has a delayed response when you move it. When surfing the Internet, Web sites take much longer to load. Your digital music or video files do not play normally. When using a word-processing program, the words you type do not appear immediately onscreen (there is noticeable lag). Or it takes an unusual amount of time to open a folder or a window.
>
> **Pesky pop-ups:** An unusually large quantity of pop-up advertisements appears while you surf the Web, or perhaps the pop-ups show up even when your computer is not connected to the Internet. Often these pop-ups are pornographic.
>
> **Home page hijack:** Without your consent, your Internet browser's "home page" (the Web site that opens up first when you run your browser) is changed. Often the new home page is for a pornographic site.
>
> **New bookmarks:** New Web links are added to your Internet browser's "bookmarks" folder (also referred to as "favorites"). Often these links are for pornographic Web sites.
>
> **Unusual icons:** Strange shortcuts known as "icons" appear on your Windows desktop. If clicked, these icons usually launch a pornographic program or send you to a pornographic Web site.

Do It Yourself

How does spyware infect a computer?

What does spyware do?

If you think your computer is infected with spyware

Anti-spyware programs

Reactive anti-spyware programs

Proactive anti-spyware programs

Automatic dialing: Without your permission, your computer attempts to connect to the Internet (via a dial-up connection).

Abnormal activity: Your modem indicates that your computer is sending and receiving large amounts of data from the Internet—even when you aren't doing anything!

Uninvited toolbars: You discover that strange "toolbars" have been added to the top of your Web browser. Usually these toolbars have unfamiliar names and are not to be trusted. However, you can trust toolbars that you intentionally downloaded from respected companies such as Google, Yahoo, and MSN.

> **It's a Fact**
> Approximately 90 percent of all computers worldwide that use the Internet have been—or currently are—infected with spyware.

How Does Spyware Infect a Computer?

There are numerous ways that spyware can sneak into your computer:

Internet advertisements: When you click a malicious pop-up ad, spyware can be downloaded to your computer.

File-sharing software: It hides inside programs used for illegally sharing MP3 music files or pirated movies. When you install the software, the spyware is installed at the same time.

Pirated software: Illegal copies of software purchased on the street or downloaded from the Internet often contain spyware.

Shareware/freeware: It can lurk inside inexpensive or free software available on the Internet from non-reputable vendors or persons.

Fake spyware-removal programs: Believe it or not, some anti-spyware programs actually install spyware. To stay safe from this scam, install only spyware-removal software that has a solid, respected reputation.

E-mail attachments: Just like a virus, spyware can be installed on your computer when you open an infected e-mail attachment.

Hackers: A hacker who has already found a way into your computer courtesy of a virus, worm, or Trojan horse can install spyware on your system.

What Does Spyware Do?

- Installs a "keystroke logging" program that allows a criminal to see everything you type on your keyboard (including passwords and credit card numbers)

- Hijacks your Internet browser and changes its default home page and search engine or both

FYI

To avoid spyware lurking in Internet ads, *never* click them. Sometimes clicking the "X" button in the upper-right corner of a pop-up ad can actually trigger a spyware installation. To safely close the pop-up, press the Ctrl key on your keyboard while simultaneously pressing the W key.

- Tracks your Internet-surfing habits and sends this information to hackers who can use it to commit identity theft, or to online marketers who will send you customized pop-up advertisements

- Hogs your system's memory, CPU cycles, and Internet bandwidth

- Creates its own files, folders, cookies, DLLs, and registry keys

If You Think Your Computer Is Infected with Spyware

Don't take chances. If your computer exhibits any of the symptoms listed at the beginning of Part III of this book, take action immediately by scanning for and removing spyware.

1. Connect to the Internet.

2. Download two different spyware-removal programs. (See the following fix titled "Anti-Spyware Programs")

3. Disconnect from the Internet.

4. Uninstall all file-sharing programs such as Kazaa, BitTorrent, Limewire, or Bearshare that are used for trading pirated MP3 files or movies. If you do not get rid of these programs, they will reinstall any spyware you remove.

    a. Click the Start button in the lower-left corner of Windows.

    b. Click the Control Panel. (If you don't see this option, then your Start menu is in classic mode. In that case, click Settings, and then select the Control Panel.)

    c. If the Control Panel is in category view, click the Add or Remove Programs category. If the Control Panel is in classic view, simply double-click the Add or Remove Programs icon.

    d. A window opens. Scroll down the list until you see the name of a file-sharing program.

    e. Click the name of the file-sharing program, and then click the Remove button on its right.

5. Install one of the anti-spyware programs you just downloaded. If you downloaded Ad-Aware, then install it first.

6. Connect to the Internet.

7. Open the anti-spyware program, and then update it (often referred to as updating its "definitions"). This ensures it is capable of removing the newest spyware threats.

8. Use the anti-spyware program to scan your *entire* computer. If it finds any spyware, make sure it removes or "quarantines" each piece.

9. If the anti-spyware program asks you to reboot your computer so it can properly remove stubborn pieces of spyware, then follow its instructions. Even if it doesn't ask you this, it is still a good idea to reboot.

10. When you return to Windows, install your second anti-spyware program.

11. Connect to the Internet.

12. Open the second anti-spyware program, and then update it.

13. Use the second anti-spyware program to scan your *entire* computer. If it finds any spyware, make sure it removes or quarantines each piece.

14. If one of your anti-spyware programs allows you to turn on "shields" to protect you from future infections, then do so.

15. If your computer still acts strangely, it might be infected with a different digital threat such as a virus, worm, or Trojan horse. Consider using antivirus software to scan for those threats. For more information on viruses, refer to Chapter 5.

16. If your computer still has problems, call Geeks On Call.

Anti-Spyware Programs

Currently no spyware-removal programs are perfect; all of them catch spyware that the others miss. Your best bet is to install two different programs and use them both to scan for and remove spyware. Anti-spyware programs fall into two categories: "reactive" and "proactive."

Reactive Anti-Spyware Programs

These programs can remove spyware that already lurks on your computer, but they have little or no capabilities to prevent future infections. Often these programs can be downloaded for free, but give you the option of adding "shields" by paying a fee or by upgrading to a "Pro" version.

- Ad-Aware Free Version (www.lavasoftusa.com)
- Spybot Search and Destroy (www.safer-networking.org)

Proactive Anti-Spyware Programs

Along with removing spyware, a proactive program can prevent most spyware from sneaking into your computer by placing virtual shields over it. These shields can halt spyware installations, protect your Internet browser's home page from being hijacked, prevent new bookmarks/favorites from being added to your Internet browser without your permission, block third-party tracking cookies, and much more. These proactive programs must be purchased from an Internet e-merchant or from a brick-and-mortar retail store.

- Spy Sweeper (www.webroot.com)
- eTrust PestPatrol (www.ca.com)
- McAfee AntiSpyware (www.mcafee.com)

7

WIRELESS THREATS

Wireless Internet. It's truly amazing, if you stop to think about it. All of those Web sites, pictures, music files, and video clips skating on sheets of air, twirling unharmed through walls and floors until they glide into your wireless computer. Musician Joey Scarbury was ahead of his time when he sang, "Believe it or not, I'm walking on air. I never thought I could feel so free." (In case that sounds familiar, it is the theme to the popular 1980s TV show The Greatest American Hero.) Indeed, the freedom of wireless devices has changed our world for the better. But like all technological marvels, such devices aren't perfect. If you don't take the proper precautions, your wireless devices can become an open invitation for high-tech thieves to waltz in and steal your data — or even your identity.

Do It Yourself

Invisible criminals

Wi-Fi hacking

Evil twin hotspots

Invasion of the data snatchers

Wireless keyboards

Cell phones

Invisible Criminals

As laptop computers have become less expensive and more powerful, greater numbers of people have cut themselves free from desktops and gone mobile. In turn, this has spurred a surge in demand for wireless Internet devices that can beam signals throughout an entire home or office. Paralleling the rise of these devices is an increase in wireless crimes with ominous names like "Wi-Fi hacking" and "evil twin hotspots."

Wi-Fi Hacking

When your family members head off to work and school in the morning, do you prop open the front door and stick a sign in your lawn that says "Burglars welcome"? Unfortunately, that's exactly what you are doing if you don't turn on the security features of your wireless Internet devices. In a crime often referred to as "Wi-Fi hacking," criminals drive through neighborhoods and business districts to see if they can access an

unprotected and unencrypted wireless computer network. If successful, they can hijack that wireless Internet connection to send spam or download illegal materials (such as child pornography). Also, intruders are only one step away from being able to hack into the victim's
computer, view private files — in particular credit card numbers and social security numbers — and use that information to commit identity theft. Here's how to lock down a wireless router:

Note

Because different brands of routers have different features, you should consult your router's manual for specific details about how to implement these tips.

Center the router: Place the router in the center of your home or office to provide equal coverage to all rooms and to prevent the majority of your signal from leaking out a window.

Change the password: Most routers come with a default password — usually "admin" — that allows you to access the router's interface and tweak its features. By creating a new, strong password, you give your router greater protection from attacks. For more information on creating strong passwords that are difficult to crack, see Chapter 16.

Update the firmware: This is a collection of special operating instructions embedded in a router's hardware. Periodically the router's manufacturer will release new versions of firmware to fix glitches, plug security holes, and offer new features. To download the most recent firmware for your device, visit the main Web site for its manufacturer and look for a link labeled Support.

Turn on encryption: By default, most routers come out of the box with their encryption capabilities turned off, which means a criminal can snatch your data out of the air. Prevent this by scrambling your signal with the WEP or WPA security protocol, usually found by accessing your router's setup software. Also, avoid using encryption keys that someone can guess (such as words or names). Instead, use a combination of random letters and numbers.

Change the SSID: The SSID is the name you give your wireless network. Typically, a manufacturer gives all of its routers the same SSID. For example, Linksys routers have an SSID of "linksys." By accessing your router's onscreen setup menu and changing your SSID, you make it more difficult for people to hack into your network. Choose a new SSID that does not identify who you are or where you are located. Instead, create one that has no direct connection to your personal information. To be even safer, change your SSID every few months.

Don't broadcast your SSID: By disabling your newly created SSID from being broadcast for all the world to see, you will make it even more difficult for an intruder to find his way into your network. Usually this feature is found in a router's onscreen setup menu.

Use "MAC Address Filtering": This feature thwarts unauthorized users from connecting to your network. Again, refer to your router's onscreen setup menu.

Turn off "DHCP": Disabling this option makes it tougher for an attacker to force his way into your network. Just like the previous options, you need to access your router's onscreen setup menu.

Evil Twin Hotspots

If you have ever watched a soap opera (come on, you can admit it!), you are probably familiar with the clichéd "evil twin" plot line. But did you know that evil twins are real? In computer terms, an evil twin is a free, wireless hotspot created by a criminal to mimic the public Internet access available at places such as Starbucks and bookstores. Usually the evil twin hotspot looks legitimate, so customers connect to it and send e-mail, surf the Web, and do online banking— without any idea that everything they do or type is being recorded by the criminal (including passwords and account numbers). Avoid becoming a victim by staying alert and following some public Wi-Fi precautions:

Disable auto log-on: Do not give your laptop permission to automatically log on to the nearest Wi-Fi hotspot.

Surf selectively: Don't visit Web sites that require sensitive information such as passwords, account numbers, and user names that could be captured by the evil twin and used to commit identity theft.

Don't use unsecure e-mail: Avoid checking e-mail from an unsecured source (such as your Internet provider). Instead, use only secure Web mail services such as Hotmail or Gmail. Also, be sure to always select the I'm Using a Public Computer option or the Always Ask for My E-Mail Address and Password option.

Use cell-phone Internet: Consider connecting your laptop to your cell phone to use its Internet connection (assuming you already signed up for this feature).

Invasion of the Data Snatchers

Wireless laptops and routers are not the only devices targeted by criminals; other gadgets such as wireless keyboards and cell phones are also at risk.

Wireless Keyboards

A keyboard freed from the confinements of a tangled cord is a boost to any cluttered desk. However, many users are not aware that unless they use encryption software, everything they type can be snatched out of the air by a savvy crook. But don't despair; this is one remedy that won't cost you a cent. Most wireless keyboards come with an installation CD containing special software that allows you to encrypt its signal. If you have lost the CD, you can download the most recent version of the software by visiting the manufacturer's Web site. A word of caution: no encryption software is perfect, so if you routinely type sensitive information on your keyboard and don't want to risk having it snatched, then use a standard wired keyboard.

Cell Phones

Despite advancements in technology, modern cell phones are not immune from intrusion by data snatchers, eavesdroppers, or computer viruses. Here's what to do:

Watch your mouth: If you need to discuss critical information over the phone — such as social security numbers, credit card numbers, or passwords — use an old-fashioned landline.

Disable Bluetooth: If your cell phone is equipped with Bluetooth technology and you don't use it, disable its features (if your phone permits). Leaving Bluetooth on could cause you to be bombarded by spammed text messages or other digital threats.

Use cell-phone antivirus software: If you have one of those fancy half-computer/half-phone devices, you might be susceptible to new cell-phone viruses that have recently emerged. Whenever possible, use an antivirus program designed especially for cell phones.

8

PHISHING SCAMS

Phishing (pronounced "fishing") is a scam that tricks people into revealing their private, personal information (such as credit card numbers and passwords).

Gone Phishing

Originally, phishing was an e-mail scam in which criminals sent a fake "urgent" message that appeared to be from a respected company or financial institution. The message asked its recipients to verify or update their account information by clicking a link in the e-mail and visiting a special Web site. When the victims followed the instructions, the information they entered on the fake Web site was captured by the criminals and used to commit identity theft. In recent years, this crime has produced several sinister spin-offs. Now, phishing is used more as a term to refer to data-mining scams in general.

Types of Phishing

E-mail links: The link sends you to a Web site that looks legitimate. When you follow the e-mail's instructions and verify or update your account information, your data is stolen and used to commit identity theft. Also, clicking the link can cause spyware or similar digital threats to be downloaded to your computer.

Instant-message links: Similar to e-mail phishing. These instant-message links are designed to look like they are from someone on your "buddy" list of contacts.

Pharming: This scam redirects you from legitimate Web sites to fake ones that look like the real deal. When you enter an ID, password, or credit card number, your information is stolen.

Do It Yourself

Gone phishing

Types of phishing

Warning signs

How to avoid phishing scams

Phishy e-mail

How to spot a fake Microsoft e-mail

Examples of fraudulent e-mail

Cross-site scripting: Criminals sabotage real Web sites and put their own log-in boxes on those sites. When you enter an ID and password into the boxes, your information is stolen.

URL hijacking: Criminals take advantage of a company's flawed or unprotected Web site address to redirect you to a phishing site.

Phone or snail-mail scams: You receive a live phone call, a voicemail, or a snail-mail letter from a criminal who claims to represent a company or financial institution that you have done business with recently. The criminal asks you to verify or update some account information.

Warning Signs

Most e-mail phishing scams have common attributes:

E-mail from well-known companies: Most legitimate companies or financial institutions will *not* contact you via e-mail to request private information or to discuss serious or urgent matters. Instead, they usually call you or send a formal letter via snail-mail.

Unprofessional e-mail: The e-mail contains horrible grammar or mistakes in spelling and punctuation.

Microsoft e-mail: Microsoft never sends software patches or updates via e-mail attachments or e-mail links. The only safe way to get these updates is to download them manually from Microsoft's Web site or turn on the Automatic Updates feature of Windows. For more information, refer to Chapter 1.

Instant-message link: You receive a link inside an instant message that claims to be from a friend or acquaintance.

How to Avoid Phishing Scams

Don't respond to e-mail asking for private information: Instead, be proactive and call the bank or company and ask them whether they are trying to get in touch with you. Most financial institutions have toll-free phone numbers you can call (usually the number is listed on the back of your credit card).

Don't click links in strange or unexpected e-mail: This is true especially for e-mail that appears to be from a financial institution.

Read your e-mail offline (disconnected from the Internet): This prevents hostile code from being downloaded to your computer if you accidentally click a phishing link in an e-mail. For dial-up users, this is easy: simply log-off your Internet service. For users of always-on, high-speed cable/DSL connections, you need to turn on the "lock" feature of your software firewall to halt all inbound and outbound Internet activity.

Don't click links inside instant messages: This is true regardless of whether or not the link was sent to you from someone on your "buddy" list of contacts.

Never send your personal or financial information in an e-mail or instant message: Don't send credit card numbers, social security numbers, bank account numbers, passwords, user names, and so on. A normal e-mail or instant message does not have encryption protection, which means it can be intercepted by a criminal who can use your private information to commit identity theft. If you need to give important information to someone, call him/her on the telephone — but use a landline because cell-phone calls can also be intercepted.

Beware of telephone phishing: Phishing scams can be committed over the telephone.

- Do not respond to voicemails from companies asking you to call a phone number to clear up information about your account. This could be phone phishing. Instead, call their central phone number and find out whether or not they really need to speak with you.

- Be suspicious of companies who call you out of the blue and ask you to verify information such as your account number, password, PIN number, mother's maiden name, social security number, age, home address, and so on. Don't tell them anything. Instead, hang up and call their central phone number.

Install an anti-phishing toolbar: A few companies offer free software toolbars that can be added to your Internet browser to protect you from accidentally visiting phishing Web sites.

- Netcraft Toolbar (http://toolbar.netcraft.com) for Internet Explorer and Firefox, free download

- TrustWatch Toolbar (www.trustwatch.com), free download

- Cloudmark SafetyBar (www.cloudmark.com) for Internet Explorer only, free download

Check the Web site's security certificate: Most e-commerce Web sites have certificates proving their Internet transactions are safe and secure. If you are ever uncertain about a site, check its security certificate.

1. If the lower-right corner of your Internet browser displays an icon that looks like a closed padlock, that means the Web site you are visiting is secure (see Figure 8-1). Double-click the padlock to view the Web site's security certificate, and then proceed to Step 8.

©2003 Microsoft Corporation. All rights reserved. Terms of Use Privacy Statement

🔒 Internet

Figure 8-1

2. If no padlock is visible on the Web site, then type **https://** into your Internet browser instead of the normal `http://`. Adding the "s" to the Web address enables you to view the secure version of a company's site.

3. After `https://` type the rest of the site's usual Web address. For example, `https://www.amazon.com`. If you are redirected to a normal `http://` site, that means a secure version is not available.

4. If you are successful in reaching the secure version, you might see a box that says `This page contains both secure and non-secure items. Do you want to display the non-secure items?` Click No.

5. If you are using Microsoft's Internet Explorer, click the File drop-down menu.

6. Select Properties.

7. A window appears. Click the word Certificates in the lower-right corner of this window.

8. In the certificate, look for the company listed under the heading labeled Issued to. If the name on the certificate matches the Web address of the site you are visiting, then the site is safe to use for e-commerce. For example, the certificate for Amazon.com says it is issued to `www.amazon.com` (see Figure 8-2). Because the name on the certificate matches the address in your Internet browser (`www.amazon.com`), the site is safe.

Figure 8-2

Phishy E-Mail

If you think there is something "phishy" about an e-mail, delete it immediately. Don't take any chances. To help you determine if a message from Microsoft or from your bank is a scam, the following fixes detail the attributes of common fakes.

How to Spot a Fake Microsoft E-Mail

Microsoft *never* sends software updates or patches via e-mail. However, sometimes it will send legitimate e-mail about other topics. To help you figure out if a Microsoft e-mail is a fake, here are some tips:

It has an attachment: A fake Microsoft e-mail will trick you into opening an attachment by claiming that it is an update for Windows or another Microsoft program.

It has bogus information: If the e-mail talks about security updates or other topics not mentioned on Microsoft's main Web site (www.microsoft.com) or on its Security Homepage (www.microsoft.com/security), then most likely it is a fake.

You are asked to click a link: A fake e-mail will try to trick you into clicking a link in the message, which can cause a digital threat to be downloaded onto your computer. Usually these bogus links claim to be from a Microsoft Web site that promises to give you information or patches for a Windows security flaw. Instead of clicking the link, visit Microsoft's Security Homepage and see for yourself whether or not the security problem is real.

The security certificate is outdated or inaccurate: If you click a link in an e-mail and are sent to a Web site, check the Web site's security certificate to see whether or not it legitimately belongs to Microsoft. If the site doesn't have a security certificate, or if the certificate has inaccurate or outdated information, then leave immediately. For more details on this process, refer to "Check the Web site's security certificate" listed earlier in this chapter (in the fix "How to Avoid Phishing Scams").

Examples of Fraudulent E-Mail

Phishing scams have been successful because they prey upon people's fear of identity fraud. As you can see by the examples that follow, the majority of these scams claim to be from reputable, national companies and use language designed to panic victims into clicking the included Web link.

Bank Of America

Subject line: "Online Banking Alert (Change of Email Address)"
Sender: Online Banking Notices (5thvtc@alert.bankofamerca.com)
    Information requested: Your Bank Of America username, password, and ATM-card information.

eBay

Subject line: "Update or verify your account information"
Sender: eBay
Message: "We have detected a slight error in your billing information . . . This might be due to either of the following reasons . . . Please update and verify your information by clicking the link below . . ."

Comcast

Subject line: "ATTENTION: Comcast account reactivation !!! ID: "
Sender: SebastianMareygrossness@comcast-support.biz
    Information requested: Your Comcast username/password, credit card information, and address.

Paypal

Subject line: "New email address added to your account"
Sender: `aw-service@paypal.com`
Message: "You have added `laptopseller@yahoo.com` as a new
email address for your PayPal account. If you did not authorize
this change or if you need assistance with your account, please
contact PayPal customer service . . ."

Amazon.com

Subject line: "Account Verification Notice"
Sender: `service@amazon.com`
Message: "During our regular update and verification of the
accounts, we couldn't verify your account information . . . Please
update and verify your information below."

MSN

Subject line: "Banking Online customer Report"
Sender: MSN Suspending Updating
Message: "During one of our regular automated verification
procedures we've encountered a some [sic] problem caused by
the fact that we could not verify the info that you provided to us.
Please, give us the following information so that we could fully
verify your identity. Otherwise your access to MSN services will
be closed."

AOL

Subject line: "Notice : Your account will be suspended !"
Sender: AOL
Message: " . . . your AOL account information needs to be updated
. . . If you could please take 5-10 minutes out of your online
experience and update your personal records you will not run into
any future problems with the online service."

Visa

Subject line: "Update or verify your account information"
Sender: Visa Service Department
Message: "To ensure your Visa card's security, it is important that
you protect your Visa card online with a personal password.
Please take a moment, and activate for Verified by Visa now."

EarthLink

Subject line: "Earthlink payment is cancelled"

Sender: support@earthlink.com

Message: "Your automatic payment was declined by your bank or credit card company. You can update your billing information or make a one-time credit card payment by answering to this email by pressing REPLY or mailing your billing details . . ."

Well-designed phishing e-mail can look 100 percent convincing. In recent years, fake Microsoft security bulletins have fooled many Windows users. When people clicked the first bulletin (Figure 8-3), it caused a worm to be downloaded to their computers. When they entered their private information into the second bulletin (Figure 8-4), they became victims of identity theft. Always use caution when reading an e-mail. When in doubt, delete it.

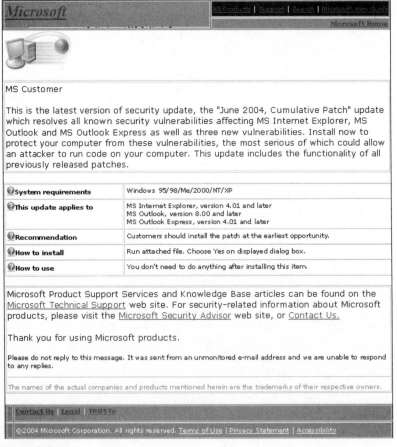

Figure 8-3

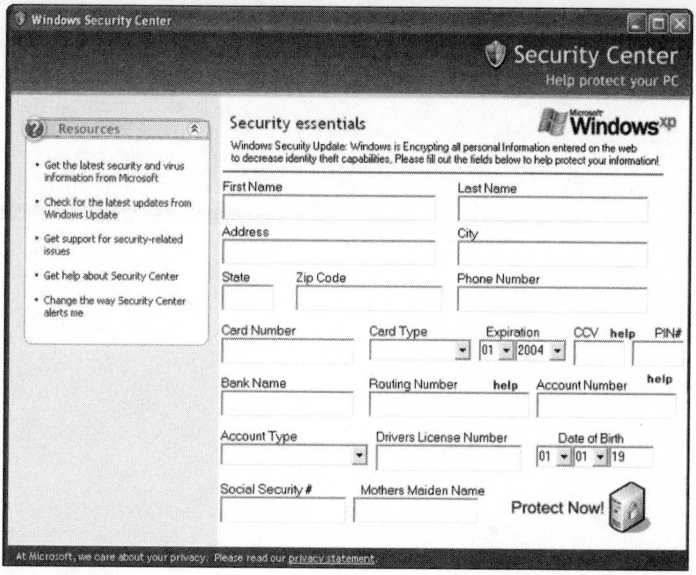
Windows Security Center
Security Center
Help protect your PC
Resources
Get the latest security and virus information from Microsoft
Check for the latest updates from Windows Update
Get support for security-related issues
Get help about Security Center
Change the way Security Center alerts me
Security essentials
Microsoft Windows xp
Windows Security Update: Windows is Encrypting all personal Information entered on the web to decrease identity theft capabilities. Please fill out the fields below to help protect your information!
First Name
Last Name
Address
City
State
Zip Code
Phone Number
Card Number
Card Type
Expiration
01
2004
CCV
help
PIN#
Bank Name
Routing Number
help
Account Number
help
Account Type
Drivers License Number
Date of Birth
01
01
19
Social Security #
Mothers Maiden Name
Protect Now!
At Microsoft, we care about your privacy. Please read our privacy statement.

Figure 8-4

9

SPAM

T hink back to what life was like before the Internet. Remember when the word "Spam" referred to an instantly recognizable tin can of processed meat found in your local grocery store? Not anymore. Today's spam has no nutritional value. In fact, it has no value at all. This new version of spam is nothing more than a collection of annoying, troublesome — and possibly dangerous — e-mail advertisements. If you use e-mail on a regular basis, you have probably received hundreds or even thousands of these unsolicited messages offering to enhance your body parts, sell you cheap Viagra, or give you mind-blowing mortgage rates. If you are tired of weeding through junk e-mail each morning, you are in luck — there are several ways to can spam.

Canning Spam

If you want to can your spam problem and reclaim your Inbox from the onslaught of ads, get-rich-quick schemes, and X-rated messages, there are several steps to take.

Note
Even the best anti-spam strategies allow an occasional spam message to slip through. None of them is perfect by itself, but when used in combination with each other, they should reduce your spam problem by 95 to 99 percent.

Never open spam: There's an old saying about food products past their expiration date: "When it doubt, throw it out." This adage is true for real Spam as well as spam e-mail. If you suspect an e-mail is spam, just delete it. Some spam are actually designed to alert their creators whenever they are opened, which lets the spammer know that your e-mail address is active and ripe for more spam. If you are tempted to open questionable e-mail because you think it is safe, you can view details about it by using the "passive viewer" of Outlook or Outlook Express. For more information, refer to Chapters 3 and 4.

Never click spam links: If you accidentally open a spam, close it immediately. And no matter what, never click any links in the spam. Doing so could cause you to become a victim of a "phishing" scam. For more information on phishing, refer to Chapter 8.

Turn on your ISP's spam filter: Not all Internet service providers (ISPs) turn on spam filters by default when you sign up with them or when you add another e-mail address to your existing account. Check with your ISP to ensure that all possible spam filters are being used.

Install anti-spam software: Numerous companies make special software that will plug into your favorite e-mail program to scan your incoming messages and block almost all spam from entering your Inbox. Here are some popular programs (in no particular order):

- ETrust Anti-Spam (www.ca.com)
- Spam Shredder (www.webroot.com)
- Norton AntiSpam (www.symantec.com)
- iHateSpam (www.sunbelt-software.com)
- McAfee SpamKiller (www.mcafee.com)
- MailWasher Pro (www.mailwasher.net)
- CYBERsitter Antispam (www.cybersitter.com)
- Cloudmark SafetyBar (www.cloudmark.com), free for Outlook and Outlook Express

Use multiple e-mail accounts: To increase your privacy and reduce spam, use multiple e-mail accounts. Keep one "good" account for e-mailing friends and family, and have a "junk" account used for Internet purchases and for documents requiring an e-mail address (from banks, credit cards, club memberships, doctors' offices, and so on). Doing so keeps your "good" address from being sold to third-party marketers. When signing up for a "junk" account, divulge as little private information as possible. That way, if your "junk" address gets passed around the Internet, your confidentiality will be protected.

Take precaution with Internet messages: If you post messages on Internet newsgroups (often referred to as the "UseNet") or on "blogs," do not include your real e-mail address with your message. Sinister programs called "spambots" scour newsgroups and blogs daily to harvest e-mail addresses to which marketers can send spam. A solution is to post messages that contain an altered version of your e-mail address along with instructions on how to decipher it. For example, you could write Reply to: bob@nospamhotmail.com and remove the "nospam".

Disable the Preview pane: In Microsoft's Outlook and Outlook Express, a split-window feature known as the Preview pane can help spammers to send you more junk mail. For instructions on disabling the Preview pane, refer to Chapters 3 and 4.

10

COOKIES

C omputer cookies are small text files that store information about the Web sites you have visited and the things you did on those sites.

Are Computer Cookies Yummy?

Sorry, these cookies can be digested only by Internet sites. Cookies come in two flavors: "trustworthy" and "tracking."

Trustworthy Cookies

These helpful cookies make your Internet experience more simple and effective. Typically, they are used for the following:

Remembering IDs and passwords: Cookies can keep track of your IDs and passwords for Web sites, which saves you the hassle of retyping them each time you visit those sites.

Assisting e-commerce: When you shop at e-tailers' Web sites, cookies keep track of the items in your virtual shopping cart and assist you in making purchases.

Personalizing Web sites: You can customize a Web site to show only the content you want to view, such as breaking news, sports scores, weather forecasts, movie showtimes, and more.

Tracking Cookies

In *Star Wars* terms, these devious cookies have joined the dark side of the Force. Most often they are used by Internet advertisers and marketers for:

Web site monitoring: Businesses track the areas of their Web sites you visit and the content you view.

Do It Yourself

Are computer cookies yummy?

Trustworthy cookies

Tracking cookies

How to control cookies

Manual deletion

For Internet Explorer

For the Firefox Web browser

Web-browser tweaks

For Internet Explorer

For Firefox

Software solutions

Online advertising: Marketers and advertisers track your Internet habits so they can show you customized advertisements based on the types of Web sites you visit and the purchases you make. Often these are referred to as "third-party" cookies.

How to Control Cookies

To protect your privacy, you should take control of the cookies on your computer. There are several methods of doing this, most of which are equally effective.

Manual Deletion

A simple way to remove tracking cookies is to delete *all* of the cookies on your computer.

Note

This also deletes trustworthy cookies, such as those used for online banking or Web e-mail.

For Internet Explorer

1. Open Internet Explorer.
2. Click the Tools drop-down menu.
3. Select Internet Options.
4. A window opens. On the General tab, look for the words Temporary Internet Files. Underneath them, click the Delete Cookies button (see Figure 10-1).

Figure 10-1

5. A window opens with the message Delete All Cookies in the Temporary Internet Files Folder?

6. Click OK.

7. If other users have a Windows account on your computer, have each of them log on to their account and repeat these steps.

For the Firefox Web Browser

1. Open Firefox.

2. Click the Tools drop-down menu.

3. Select Options.

4. A window opens. In the left window pane, click the padlock icon that says Privacy.

5. In the right window pane, look for the word Cookies. On its right, click the Clear button (see Figure 10-2).

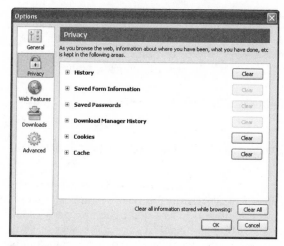

Figure 10-2

6. If other users have a Windows account on your computer, have each of them log on to their account and repeat these steps.

Web-Browser Tweaks

Popular Web browsers such as Internet Explorer or Firefox allow you to change their settings for handling cookies.

For Internet Explorer

1. Open Internet Explorer.

2. Click the Tools drop-down menu.

3. Select Internet Options.

4. Click the Privacy tab.

5. Click the Advanced button.

6. Put a checkmark in the Override automatic cookie handling box (see Figure 10-3).

Figure 10-3

7. Under First-party Cookies heading, click the Block button.

8. Below this, check the Always allow session cookies box. This allows Web sites to place a cookie on your computer that will expire the moment you exit the site (which means the cookie cannot be used to track you).

9. Under the heading Third-party Cookies, click the Block button.

10. Click OK.

11. Now you should be back at the Privacy screen. Click the Sites button.

12. A window opens. In the center of it are the words Address of Web site, beneath which is a blank box. In this box, type the address of trustworthy Web sites that need cookies to function properly (Web e-mail services such as Hotmail, financial institutions such as your bank or credit card company, e-merchants such as Amazon.com or eBay, and so on); then click the Allow button (see Figure 10-4).

Figure 10-4

13. Next, type the address of any Web sites you do not want to receive cookies from (online advertisers such as doubleclick.net, gambling sites, and so on); then click the Block button.

14. If you ever change your mind about a Web site and want to remove it from this list, simply highlight its name, click the Remove button, and then click OK.

15. When you are finished adding or removing Web sites, click OK.

For Firefox

1. Open Firefox.

2. Click the Tools drop-down menu.

3. Select Options.

4. A window opens. In the left window pane, click the padlock icon labeled Privacy.

5. Click the word Cookies.

6. Put a checkmark in the Allow sites to set cookies box.

7. Underneath it, put a checkmark in the For the originating web site only box (see Figure 10-5). This prevents third-party cookies from being placed on your computer.

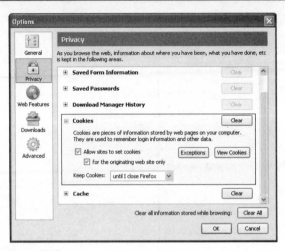

Figure 10-5

8. To create a customized list of Web sites that should always be allowed to leave cookies or should always be blocked from leaving cookies, click the Exceptions button.

9. A window opens. In the blank, type the complete address of a Web site. Click the Block button to prevent the site from ever placing cookies on your computer, or click the Allow button to give it permission to always place cookies (see Figure 10-6).

Figure 10-6

10. Click OK.

Software Solutions

Another method of removing and blocking third-party tracking cookies is to use special software:

> **Cookie programs:** They are rare, but a few programs exist that specialize in controlling cookies. Two such programs are Cookie Crusher (www.limitsoftware.com) and Window Washer (www.webroot.com).

Note

Cookie Crusher will likely slow down your Internet connection because it uses a "proxy" to filter cookies. If that is a concern, you should consider using another program.

> **Firewalls:** Many popular firewalls (both the hardware and software varieties) allow you to block cookies. In particular, some software firewalls, such as ZoneAlarm Pro, give you advanced options about which types of cookies you want to keep or reject. For more information, see Chapter 11.

> **Anti-spyware programs:** Your best bet is to install a reputable anti-spyware program. Almost all spyware removers delete tracking cookies, and most "proactive" anti-spyware programs have the added benefit of placing a shield over your computer to prevent tracking cookies from sneaking in. For more information, refer to Chapter 6.

PART IV
INTERNET SECURITY

What a Tangled Web We Weave . . .

The World Wide Web. Truly there is no better name for what we commonly call
the Internet. Weaving complex threads of simple ones and zeros that stretch from
Kalamazoo to Kathmandu, the Web "surrounds us and penetrates us . . . it binds
the galaxy together." (Yes, those words were borrowed from Obi-Wan Kenobi in
Star Wars Episode IV: A New Hope.) But the Web also evokes images of an intri-
cate trap that ensnares unsuspecting victims. Without proper precautions and
protection, modern Internet surfers can be caught in a tangled web of hackers,
thieves, and high-tech hooligans.

11

SAFE WEB SURFING

5-Minute Fixes™

I n addition to performing the fixes listed in Chapters 5 through 10, you can dramatically improve the safety and security of your Web surfing by tweaking Windows and Internet Explorer, installing special hardware and software, and following some simple guidelines.

Update Windows: Prevent digital threats such as worms and hackers from invading your computer by plugging the holes in Windows. You can manually download the security patches or you can configure Windows to automatically download and install them for you. For more information, refer to Chapter 1.

Update Microsoft Office: Similar to Windows, the Microsoft Office programs (Word, Excel, Access, PowerPoint, and so on) need to be updated with the most recent security patches. For more information, refer to Chapter 1.

Use a firewall: To protect your computer from Internet intruders, it is crucial to use a firewall. Available in hardware and software versions, a firewall acts like a cloaking device to hide your computer from the watchful eyes of online criminals. A firewall also can filter the data that enters your computer, control Internet cookies, and warn you when sinister spyware programs try to transmit data about you over the Web. There are numerous, respected brands of hardware or software firewalls to choose from, each of which will probably suit your needs.

Do It Yourself

Hardware firewalls

Software firewalls

Free firewalls

Retail firewalls

Don't use Internet Connection Sharing

Secure your router

Surf cautiously

Block pop-ups

Test your firewall

Consider other browsers

Tweak Internet Explorer

Create a custom security level

Add trusted sites

Disable AutoComplete

Block cookies

Configure advanced options

Tweak Firefox

Note

For enhanced protection, use a hardware firewall in combination with a software firewall. If you have two or more computers networked together, using dual firewalls should stop one of the computers from spreading a worm across the network and infecting the other computers. Even if you have only one computer, using both types of firewalls together won't harm anything and will give you increased protection and control over the type of information your computer broadcasts over the Web.

> **Tweak your Web browser:** All Web browsers allow you to change their security settings to increase or decrease your level of protection.

Hardware Firewalls

Hardware firewalls are available as standalone devices that sit between your computer and the Internet, and they come as a built-in feature of most routers (which are devices used to network computers together to share files and an Internet connection). Even if you have only one computer in your home or office, a router is a good, inexpensive investment because you never know when you're going to purchase an additional computer and want to set up a network. Here are some popular brands of routers (in no particular order):

- Linksys BEFSR41 or BEFSX41
- NetGear RP614
- D-Link DI-604

Software Firewalls

In addition to offering many of the same features as a hardware firewall, a software firewall can alert you when a digital threat such as spyware tries to connect to the Internet and transmit your data to online marketers. Also, most software firewalls let you choose which programs can or cannot access the Web. Many reputable software manufacturers have software firewalls available.

Free Firewalls

> **Windows Firewall:** A reliable, free firewall known as Windows Firewall is included with Windows XP Service Pack 2. If your computer does not have any other software firewall installed, then Windows Firewall automatically and silently runs in the background to protect you. Determine if your version of Windows has the Windows Firewall by following these steps:
>
> 1. Click the Start button in the lower-left corner of Windows.
>
> 2. Click the Control Panel. (If you don't see this option, then your Start menu is in classic mode. In that case, click Settings, and then select the Control Panel.)

3. If the Control Panel is in category view, click the category labeled Network and Internet Connections, and then look for an icon labeled Windows Firewall. If the Control Panel is in classic view, look for an icon labeled Windows Firewall (see Figure 11-1).

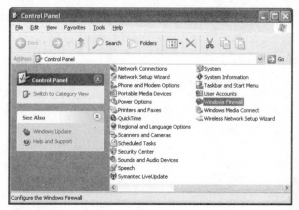

Figure 11-1

4. If the Windows Firewall is not available, then you need to install Service Pack 2. For information on how to update Windows in order to receive Service Pack 2, refer to Chapter 1.

Note

Windows Firewall will sufficiently protect you from inbound threats that attempt to penetrate your computer, but it will not alert you about any outbound threats that try to use your Internet connection. For that reason, it is not recommended.

ZoneAlarm Free Version: This is one of the best software firewalls — and it is completely free. Not only does it protect against inbound and outbound threats, but it also gives you total command over the programs that are allowed to access the Internet. To download it, visit www.zonelabs.com or search for it at www.download.com.

Retail Firewalls

- ZoneAlarm Pro (www.zonelabs.com)
- Norton Internet Security (www.symantec.com)
- McAfee Personal Firewall (www.mcafee.com)
- Tiny Personal Firewall (www.tinysoftware.com)
- Desktop Firewall (www.webroot.com)
- ETrust EZ Firewall (www.ca.com)

Don't Use Internet Connection Sharing

Recent versions of Windows offer a feature called *Internet Connection Sharing* (ICS) that allows a computer to share its Internet connection with other computers in the same home or office. Although ICS is well-intentioned, it is not as fast or secure as a hardware router. If you need to share files or an Internet connection between two or more computers, avoid ICS and use a router instead.

Secure Your Router

A fresh-out-of-the-box router typically has many of its security features disabled. If you recently installed a new router or just never got around to tweaking your older one, you can substantially raise your protection with a few simple steps.

Note
The following tips are intentionally generic because routers' features vary from manufacturer to manufacturer. For specific details on how to implement these tips, please consult your router's manual.

Change the password: Most routers comes with a default password — usually "admin" — that allows you to access the router's interface and tweak its features. By creating a new, strong password, you will give your router greater protection from Internet intruders. For more information on creating strong passwords that are difficult to crack, see Chapter 16.

Download the newest firmware: Hardware devices such as routers have special operating instructions embedded in them known as firmware. Periodically, the hardware's manufacturer will release new versions of firmware to fix glitches, plug security holes, and offer new features. To download the most recent firmware, visit the main Web site for your router's manufacturer and look for a link labeled Support.

Disable remote administration: This feature allows you to access your router and change its settings by using a computer located outside your network. It is unlikely you will ever need to do this, so go ahead and disable it. Doing so will create another layer of protection against hackers.

Perform additional tweaks: If your router has security features for "port locking" and "stealth mode," then enable both. These options may have a slightly different name depending on which router you use, so consult your manual.

Surf Cautiously

One of the easiest ways to stay safe on the Internet is to be selective about the Web sites you visit. Mainstream or commercial Web sites such as CNN.com, ESPN.com, and Amazon.com are almost always safe and have no spyware, adware, or other digital threats. However, the same cannot be said for Web sites that are off the beaten path. Generally, the sites that pose the greatest threats to you are ones devoted to pornographic materials, gambling, and pirated music or movies. In fact, many of them install adware or spyware onto your computer to advertise their products.

Block Pop-Ups

Make your Internet experience faster, safer, and less cluttered by using a pop-up blocker. This simple tool prevents your computer from being bombarded with endless, annoying Web advertisements. This is one of the easiest things you can do to reduce online hassles — and it won't cost you a cent!

> **Built-in blockers:** The latest releases of popular Web browsers such as Internet Explorer, Firefox, and Opera have pop-up blockers built into them. If your browser is outdated, this is a great reason to upgrade.

Note

To use Internet Explorer's pop-up blocker, you must install Service Pack 2 from the Windows Update Web site. For more information, refer to Chapter 1.

> **Toolbars:** Several reputable companies offer free toolbars that hook into your Web browser to block pop-ups and provide Internet search capabilities.
>
> * Yahoo Toolbar (http://toolbar.yahoo.com); also has an anti-spyware feature known as Anti-Spy
>
> * MSN Toolbar (http://toolbar.msn.com)
>
> * Google Toolbar (http://toolbar.google.com)

Test Your Firewall

Several Web sites offer free online scanners that will test a firewall to check for holes or leaks. After installing a firewall, you should consider testing it, if only to give yourself peace of mind.

* Symantec Security Check (http://security.symantec.com)
* GRC ShieldsUP! (https://www.grc.com/x/ne.dll?bh0bkyd2)
* Sygate Online Services (http://scan.sygatetech.com)
* Audit My PC (www.auditmypc.com)
* PC Flank (www.pcflank.com)
* SecurityMetrics (www.securitymetrics.com/portscan.adp)

Consider Other Browsers

Despite the popularity of Microsoft's Internet Explorer browser (used by approximately 85 percent of all Web surfers), it has been heavily criticized in recent years because numerous security flaws have been discovered. Microsoft has always been quick to patch the flaws, but its critics still insist that Internet Explorer is unsafe and should be ditched in favor of an alternate browser. What these critics seem to forget is that any Web browser used by the majority of people worldwide will automatically be the main target for Internet criminals. If another browser suddenly became king of the hill, then it too would find itself in the crosshairs of criminals. Still, you may want to consider using an alternate browser. If so, here are two solid options:

Firefox (www.mozilla.org/products/firefox)

- A free browser that is not integrated with Windows, which helps to prevent viruses and hackers from causing damage if they somehow manage to compromise Firefox.

- No support for VBScript and ActiveX (two technologies that are the reasons for many security holes in Internet Explorer).

- No spyware or adware can automatically install in Firefox just by visiting a Web site.

- Built-in pop-up blocker.

- Gives you complete control over cookies.

Opera (www.opera.com)

- Free version has advertising banners. The paid version removes the banners, gives access to e-mail support, and provides six months of free Opera Web Mail.

- Uses tabbed browsing.

- Built-in pop-up blocker.

- Appearance can be changed with different "skins."

- Voice-command feature lets you surf the Internet by using your voice and allows Web sites to be read aloud to you (for Windows XP and Windows 2000 only).

Note

If you switch browsers, you may also want to consider switching the software you use to send and receive e-mail. The creators of Firefox have an e-mail program named Thunderbird that has received positive reviews from critics and Internet users alike. Similarly, the Opera browser comes with an integrated e-mail program.

Tweak Internet Explorer

You can enhance and increase the security of Internet Explorer in several ways: change the security level, add trusted sites, disable AutoComplete, block cookies, and configure advanced options.

Create a Custom Security Level

If you want complete control over the safety of Internet Explorer, you can create a custom security level.

1. Open Internet Explorer.

2. Click the Tools drop-down menu.

3. Select Internet Options.

4. Click the Security tab.

5. Click the Custom Level button.

6. The Security Setting window opens. If you have Windows XP Service Pack 2 installed, scroll down until you see the words Automatic Prompting for File Downloads. Select Enable.

7. For maximum protection from digital threats, you should disable all features related to ActiveX controls and Java scripts.

Warning

Disabling the features related to ActiveX controls and Java scripts can interfere with the way you view and use certain Web sites. To fix this problem, you must tell Internet Explorer to trust those sites by adding them to your list of Trusted Sites.

8. Under the ActiveX Controls and Plug-ins heading, click the Disable button for each of these options (see Figure 11-2).

Figure 11-2

- Download signed ActiveX controls
- Download unsigned ActiveX controls
- Initialize and script ActiveX controls not marked as safe
- Run ActiveX controls and plug-ins
- Script ActiveX controls marked safe for scripting

9. Under the Microsoft VM heading, look for a subheading labeled Java Permissions. Beneath it, click the High Safety button.

10. Under the Miscellaneous heading, click the Disable button for each of these options:

- Access Data Sources Across Domains
- Allow META REFRESH
- Display Mixed Content
- Installation of Desktop Items
- Launching Programs and Files in an IFRAME
- Navigate Sub-Frames across Different Domains
- Userdata Persistence

11. Under the Scripting heading, click the Disable button for each of these options:

- Active Scripting
- Scripting of Java Programs
- Allow Paste Operations via Script

12. Under the User Authentication heading, look for the Logon subheading. Beneath it, click the Prompt for User Name and Password button.

13. At the bottom of the Security Settings window, click OK.

Alternate Solution: Choose a Default Security Level

The easiest way to increase the safety of Internet Explorer is to use one of its preconfigured security levels.

1. Open Internet Explorer.

2. Click the Tools drop-down menu.

3. Select Internet Options.

4. Click the Security tab.

5. In the center of the window, look for the words Security Level for This Zone. If you don't see them, click the Default Level button.

6. You will see a vertical slider (shown in the following figure) that allows you to choose an Internet security level: Low, Medium-Low, Medium, or High. For maximum protection, choose High. *Warning:* Doing this could interfere with the way you view and use certain Web sites. To fix this problem, you must tell Internet Explorer to trust those sites by adding them to your list of Trusted Sites. For more information, refer to the "Add Trusted Sites" fix in this chapter.

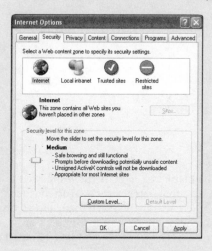

Add Trusted Sites

If you chose the High security level, some of your favorite Web sites may not function properly. To fix this problem, you must tell Internet Explorer to trust those sites.

1. Open Internet Explorer.

2. Click the Tools drop-down menu.

3. Select Internet Options.

4. Click the Security tab.

5. Click the Trusted sites icon that resembles a green checkmark (see Figure 11-3).

Figure 11-3

6. Click the Sites button.

7. Another window opens. In the blank box, type **https://** followed by the address of a commercial Web site that can always be trusted, such as your bank, credit-card company, e-merchants, Web mail, and so on (see Figure 11-4). Be sure to include the "s" after "http." For example, you type `https://www.hotmail.com` to make Hotmail a trusted site.

Figure 11-4

8. Click the Add button to place the Web site in your list of Trusted Sites.

9. Repeat this process until you have included all of the Web sites you trust.

10. To include non-secure Web sites that begin with the standard `http:` remove the checkmark from the box labeled Require server verification (`https:`) for all sites in this zone.

11. Type the address of the non-secure Web site into the box.

12. Click the Add button.

13. When you are completely finished, click OK.

14. If you ever change your mind and want to remove a Web site from this list, simply highlight its name, click Remove, and then click OK.

Disable AutoComplete

A feature called AutoComplete offers to save your Web site passwords so you don't have to retype them every time you visit those sites. This could be a serious security hazard because if a savvy hacker slips past your computer's defenses, he or she would have your list of passwords at his fingertips. Protect yourself by disabling AutoComplete:

1. Click the Start button in the lower-left corner of Windows.

2. Click the Control Panel. (If you don't see this option, then your start menu is in classic mode. In that case, click Settings, and then select the Control Panel.)

3. If the Control Panel is in category view, click the Network And Internet Connections category, and then click the icon labeled Internet Options. If the Control Panel is in classic view, simply double-click the icon labeled Internet Options.

4. A window opens. Click the Content tab (see Figure 11-5).

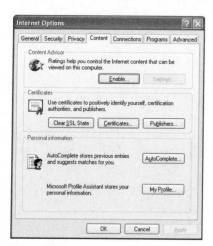

Figure 11-5

5. Click the AutoComplete button.

6. Remove the checkmarks from the three boxes labeled Web addresses, Forms, and User names and passwords on forms (see Figure 11-6).

Figure 11-6

7. Click the Clear Forms and Clear Passwords buttons. This deletes all passwords or other information that AutoComplete had previously saved.

8. Click OK.

Block Cookies

To reduce the possibility of being spied on by Internet marketers and Web sites, you can block unwanted cookies. For more information on cookies and other methods of controlling them, refer to Chapter 10.

1. Open Internet Explorer.

2. Click the Tools drop-down menu.

3. Select Internet Options.

4. Click the Privacy tab.

5. Click the Advanced button.

6. Put a checkmark in the box labeled Override automatic cookie handling (see Figure 11-7).

Figure 11-7

7. Under the First-party Cookies heading, click the Block button.

8. Below this, put a checkmark in the box labeled Always allow session cookies. This allows Web sites to place a cookie on your computer that will expire the moment you exit the site (which means the cookie cannot be used to track you).

9. Under the Third-party Cookies heading, click the Block button.

10. Click OK.

11. Now you should be back at the Privacy screen. Click the Sites button.

12. A window opens. In the center of it are the words Address of Web site, beneath which is a blank box. In this box, type the address of trustworthy Web sites that need cookies to function properly (Web e-mail services such as Hotmail, financial institutions such as your bank or credit-card company, e-merchants such as Amazon.com, eBay, and so on), and then click the Allow button.

13. Type the address of any Web sites you do not want to receive cookies from (online advertisers such as doubleclick.net, gambling sites, and so on); then click the Block button.

14. If you ever change your mind about a Web site and want to remove it from this list, simply highlight its name, click the Remove button, and then click OK.

15. When you are finished adding or removing Web sites, click OK.

Configure Advanced Options

You can give Internet Explorer even greater protection by tweaking several of its advanced options.

1. Open Internet Explorer.

2. Click the Tools drop-down menu.

3. Select Internet Options.

4. Click the Advanced tab.

5. Scroll through the list and place a checkmark in the box next to each of these options (see Figure 11-8):

  • Automatically check for Internet Explorer updates

  • Check for publisher's certificate revocation

  • Check for signatures on downloaded programs

  • Do not save encrypted pages to disk

  • Empty temporary Internet files when browser is closed

- Use SSL 2.0
- Use SSL 3.0
- Warn about invalid site certificates

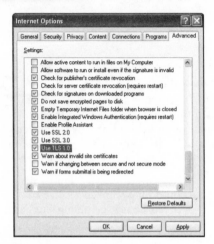

Figure 11-8

6. Scroll through the same list and remove the checkmark from each of these options:

- Enable Install on Demand (Internet Explorer)
- Enable Install on Demand (Other)
- Use inline AutoComplete
- Enable Profile Assistant

Tweak Firefox

Just like Internet Explorer, the Firefox browser allows you to customize its security settings for a better, safer online experience.

1. Open Firefox.

2. Click the Tools drop-down menu.

3. Select Options.

4. A window opens. In the left window pane, click the icon labeled General.

5. In the right window pane, click the Default Browser heading.

6. Put a checkmark in the Firefox should check to see if it is the default browser when starting box (see Figure 11-9).

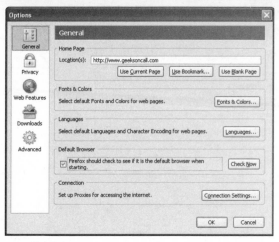

Figure 11-9

7. In the left window pane, click the icon labeled Privacy.

8. In the right window pane, click the History heading.

9. You will see the words Remember visited pages for the past 3 days. Change the number to 0 days (see Figure 11-10).

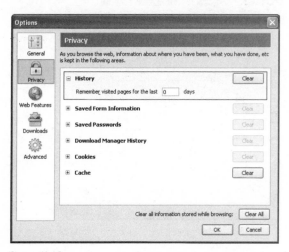

Figure 11-10

10. In the right window pane, click the Saved Form Information heading.

11. Remove the checkmark from the box labeled Save information I enter in web page forms and the Search Bar (see Figure 11-11).

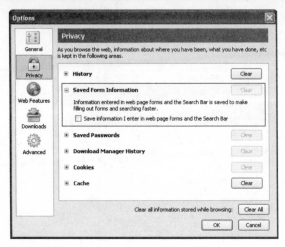

Figure 11-11

12. In the right window pane, click the Saved Passwords heading.

13. Remove the checkmark from the Remember Passwords box (see Figure 11-12).

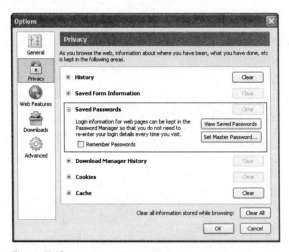

Figure 11-12

14. In the right window pane, click the Download Manager History heading.

15. Next to the words Remove files from the Download Manager, use the drop-down menu to select When Firefox exits (see Figure 11-13).

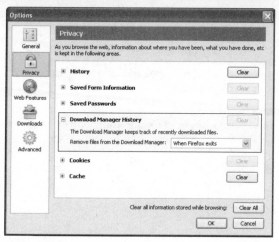

Figure 11-13

16. In the right window pane, click the Cookies heading.

17. Put a checkmark in the Allow sites to set cookies box. Underneath it, put a checkmark in the For the originating web site only box (see Figure 11-14). This prevents third-party cookies from being placed on your computer.

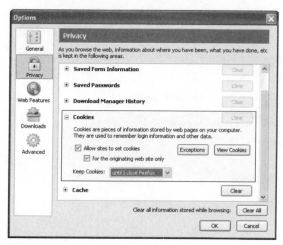

Figure 11-14

18. You can create a customized list of Web sites that should always be allowed or always be blocked from leaving cookies.

    a. Click the Exceptions button.

    b. A window opens. In the blank, type the complete address of a Web site (for example, `http://www.website.com`).

    c. Click the Block button to prevent the site from ever placing cookies on your computer, or click the Allow button to give it permission to always place cookies (see Figure 11-15).

Figure 11-15

19. In the left window pane, click the Web Features icon.

20. In the right window pane, put a checkmark in the Block Popup Windows box (see Figure 11-16).

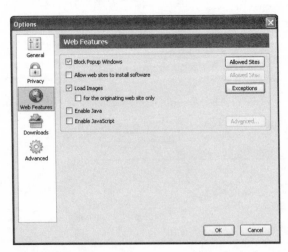

Figure 11-16

21. Remove the checkmark from the Allow Web sites to install software box.

22. Place a checkmark in the Load Images box.

23. Uncheck the Enable Java box.

Warning

Doing this could interfere with the way you view and use certain Web sites. To restore Java functionality, reverse this step and put a checkmark back in the box.

24. In the left window pane, click the Advanced icon.

25. In the right window pane, scroll down and find the Software Update heading. Under the words Periodically check for updates to, put a checkmark in the Firefox box, and then put a checkmark in the My Extensions and Themes box (see Figure 11-17).

Figure 11-17

26. Beneath this, in the Security section, make sure there are checkmarks in the Use SSL 2.0, Use SSL 3.0, and Use TLS 1.0 boxes.

12

SAFE INSTANT MESSAGING

Sending instant messages (IMs) to friends and family is a great way to stay in touch without incurring costly phone charges. However, like any Internet technology, there are several rules you should consider to protect yourself and prevent your private information from being snatched by snooping criminals.

Send IMs only to people you know: Being selective about the people you talk to prevents unwanted intruders from barging into your conversations.

Block strangers: Configure your IM program to block messages from anyone who is not on your contact/buddy list. For instructions on doing this, please consult the help menu in your IM software.

Guard your identity: Never give out credit card numbers, social security numbers, Web site passwords, security codes, IDs, or other private information. Just remember that unless you encrypt your IMs, the possibility exists for a criminal to intercept and read them.

Never click links: Don't click Web links in an IM, even if they are sent by friends or family members. It is possible that an Internet virus or worm hijacked their computer and sent you a link hoping to infect you as well.

Don't open attachments: You may trust the person sending you an IM attachment, but don't be lulled into a false sense of security. If a newly created virus is hiding in the attachment, it can slip past your virus scanner and infect your computer. Your best bet is to steer clear of all IM attachments.

In public, avoid auto log-ins: When using IM on a public computer, make sure you do not use the program's automatic log-in feature. This will prevent someone from accidentally or purposefully logging in to your account.

Use caution at work: Many companies today screen their employees' e-mail and IMs. If you don't want your boss to read your private messages, then wait and send them when you get home.

Don't forget to log off: When you are finished with an IM session, always log off. This is also true if you are going to be away from your computer for more than a few minutes. Logging off closes access ports on your computer and makes it more difficult for Internet intruders to find a way into your system.

FYI

Spim is on the rise! So what exactly is it? Spim is an unsolicited advertisement sent to you in an instant message (hence the nickname, which is a combination of spam and IM). To stamp out spim, configure your IM program to block all messages from people who are not on your contact/ buddy list.

13

SAFE CHATTING

Internet chat rooms can be a fun place to talk with other people who share your interests. But be careful: Chat-room participants often mask their true identities and might be criminals in disguise. Chat safely by following a few simple guidelines.

Choose a generic nickname: Most chat rooms ask you to create a nickname. Always use one that is generic or common and doesn't reveal personal details about yourself. For example, instead of using a nickname that identifies you and your whereabouts — such as "BostonBob" — choose a generic one such as "FootballFan."

Be anonymous: When chatting, never give out personal information that could identify you, such as your real name, address, phone number, school, place of employment, credit card numbers, social security number, pet's name, and so on.

Avoid private chats: Don't talk with someone in a private chat room. Stay safe by staying in the open.

Never meet in person: No matter how much you enjoy talking to people in a chat room, never agree to meet them in real life. The risks are too great, and you could become the victim of a serious or deadly crime.

14

SAFE
E-SHOPPING

I n recent years, the popularity of shopping on the Internet has exploded, due in large part to the convenience, vast selection, and low prices that e-merchants have compared to their brick-and-mortar counterparts (as well as no crowds and no waiting in line!). To ensure the safety of your e-shopping, you should form some good habits.

Look for the padlock: Before typing your credit card numbers into an e-merchant's Web site, look in the lower-right corner of your Web browser for an icon that looks like a closed padlock (see Figure 14-1). Its presence indicates that the Web site has proper security and encryption.

Figure 14-1

Protect your checking account: When shopping online, never use a debit card, check card, or any other card that links directly to your checking account. This will protect your account from being wiped clean by an Internet criminal who steals your identity. Although most debit/check cards claim to provide 100 percent protection in the event of identity fraud, it can take several hours or days for the money to be replaced in your checking account (especially if you have to fight with the bank to prove you didn't make the fraudulent purchases). During that time, it is possible that checks you recently wrote could bounce, and current credit transactions could be declined. For maximum protection, use a standard credit card that is not connected to your bank accounts.

Use one card: To make it easier to keep track of your Internet purchases and to spot fraud, use only one credit card for all of your e-commerce activity.

Use virtual accounts: Some credit card companies offer "virtual account numbers" that link directly to your credit card and expire as soon as they are used. By using a different virtual account each time you make an Internet purchase, you will protect your real credit card number from landing in the hands of online crooks.

15

WEB SAFETY FOR KIDS

The Internet can be a wonderful research tool and an educational resource for school-age children. However, there are many Web sites that kids should be prohibited from visiting and certain activities they should avoid. Here are some suggestions to help your kids surf safely.

Create Separate Accounts (Windows XP Home/Pro only)

If you use Windows XP, it is easy to create a separate "limited" account for your children that will prohibit them from changing system settings and installing new hardware or software. In addition, you can customize their account (including their Web browser) to protect them from harmful Internet content.

1. Click the Start button in the lower-left corner of Windows.

2. Click the Control Panel. (If you don't see this option, then your Start menu is in classic mode. In that case, click Settings, and then select the Control Panel.)

3. If the Control Panel is in category view, click the User Accounts category. If the Control Panel is in classic view, simply double-click the User Accounts icon.

4. A window opens. Click Create a New Account.

5. In the blank box, type a name for the account. For example, you can name it after one of your children or simply call it "Kids" (see Figure 15-1).

Do It Yourself

Create separate accounts (Windows XP Home/Pro only)

Establish boundaries

Block Web sites and content

Use the Content Advisor

Content-filtering software

Follow their tracks

Teach them safe chatting

Practice safe instant messaging

Figure 15-1

6. Click Next.

7. Click the Limited button, and then click the Create Account button.

Establish Boundaries

Decide what Web sites and content you feel comfortable letting your children see, and then take steps to filter or block everything else.

Block Web Sites and Content

To prevent your children from accessing Web sites with inappropriate material, you can use Internet Explorer's Content Advisor or install content-filtering software.

Use the Content Advisor

Internet Explorer has a feature known as the Content Advisor that enables you to control the Web content your children view. Similar to the "V-chip" in modern televisions, the Content Advisor uses a ratings system to help you set the level of language, nudity, sex, and violence that is acceptable in your home.

1. Open Internet Explorer.

2. Click the Tools drop-down menu.

3. Select Internet Options.

4. Click the Content tab.

5. Under the Content Advisor heading, click the Enable button (see Figure 15-2).

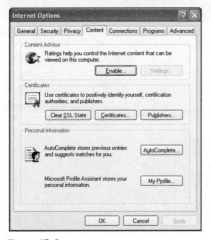

Figure 15-2

6. A window opens. Look for the words Select a category to view the ratings levels. Below them are four categories: Language, Nudity, Sex, and Violence. You can restrict Internet Explorer from accessing content in these categories by using the slider. By moving the slider all the way to the left, you enable maximum protection in the selected category. To lower the protection, move the bar to the right and choose a different level (see Figure 15-3).

Note

As the levels increase, the protection decreases.

Figure 15-3

7. Staying in the same Content Advisor window, click the Approved Sites tab. This section allows you to create a list of Web sites that your children can always view or never view regardless of the restriction level you chose in the previous step. Simply type the name of a Web site into the blank, and then either click the Always button or the Never button (see Figure 15-4). If you ever change your mind and want to remove a site from this list, simply highlight it and click the Remove button.

Figure 15-4

8. Click the General tab. Here you can choose whether or not to allow your kids to view Web sites that do not have a content rating (see Figure 15-5).

Figure 15-5

Also, you have the option to allow your children to view restricted content only if they type the proper password. To create a password:

a. Click the Create Password button.

b. A window opens into which you should type a password as well as a hint to help your children remember the password.

c. When you're finished, click OK.

d. Click the Advanced tab. Here you have the option to use a ratings bureau or PICSRules to filter Web content (see Figure 15-6).

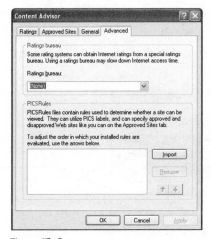

Figure 15-6

e. When you are completely finished adjusting all of the settings for the Content Advisor, click Apply.

f. Click OK.

Content-Filtering Software

Although the Content Advisor is helpful, many parents prefer to use special content-filtering software that gives them even greater control over the Web sites their children view. Here are some popular content-filtering programs (in no particular order):

- Net Nanny (www.netnanny.com)

- Cyber Patrol (www.cyberpatrol.com)

- CYBERsitter (www.cybersitter.com)

- Crayon Crawler (www.crayoncrawler.com)

- ENUFF PC (www.enuffpc.com)

- WallFly (www.smartguardsoftware.com)

Many Internet service providers (ISPs) offer special filtered Internet access programs.

Follow Their Tracks

Learn what sites your children have visited by reviewing their Internet history.

For Internet Explorer

1. Open Internet Explorer.

2. Click the History button (which resembles a circular arrow).

3. A vertical window opens on the left side of Internet Explorer. Click the day of the week you want to search.

4. Scroll down the list to see the names of the Web sites your children viewed (see Figure 15-7).

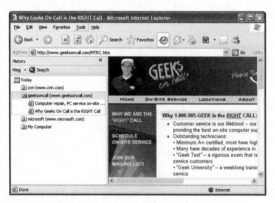

Figure 15-7

5. To visit one of the sites, click its name. A sublist opens containing links to specific pages from that site. Click a link to go directly to that page.

For Firefox

1. Open Firefox.

2. Click the Go drop-down menu.

3. Select History.

4. A vertical window opens on the left side of Firefox. Click the day of the week you want to search.

5. Scroll down the list to see the names of the Web pages your children viewed (see Figure 15-8).

Figure 15-8

6. To visit one of the pages, click its name.

Teach Them Safe Chatting

Because many chat rooms are havens for sexual predators, you should oversee your children's participation and keep them away from any chat rooms that are not moderated by trustworthy adults. Along with teaching your kids the safety guidelines listed in Chapter 13, you should warn them about the dangers of sending photos of themselves to anyone they meet in a chat room or agreeing to call or visit the person in real life.

Practice Safe Instant Messaging

After reviewing with your children the IM safety guidelines listed in Chapter 12, be sure to stress to them the importance of never opening IM attachments and never clicking on links in an IM.

PART V

DATA SECURITY

The Digital You

From vacation photos to work-related documents, the files stored on your computer are an extension of your personality. It's almost like having a digital twin sitting on your hard drive. (Suddenly the movie *Tron* comes to mind.) This is the reason cyber-criminals go to such great lengths to break into your computer. To them, it is like a bank vault full of cash and precious jewels that has been left wide open with no security guards in sight. Slam the door shut on these intruders by safeguarding your computer data and protecting the digital you.

16

PASSWORDS AND PRIVACY

In the classic tale *Ali Baba and the 40 Thieves*, the door to a secret treasure cave is opened by speaking the magic words "Open Sesame." Your computer is much like that cave — full of valuable information that is like gold to a criminal. To protect your digital treasures, turn on the privacy features of Windows and use passwords with your Windows accounts. For further protection, use passwords with your computer's hardware, such as a motherboard or router.

Disable the Welcome Screen (Windows XP Home/Pro only)

The Welcome screen is a default feature in Windows XP Home Edition and XP Professional Edition that allows you to log on to Windows by simply clicking the picture that corresponds to your account. To make Windows XP even safer from unauthorized intruders, you can disable the Welcome screen, which means that all users on your computer must manually type their account name (as well as their password, if they have one) to gain entrance to Windows.

1. Click the Start button in the lower-left corner of Windows.

2. Click the Control Panel. (If you don't see this option, then your Start menu is in classic mode. In that case, click Settings, and then select the Control Panel.)

3. If the Control Panel is in category view, click the User Accounts category. If the Control Panel is in classic view, simply double-click the User Accounts icon.

4. A window opens. Under the Pick a Task heading, click the words Change the Way Users Log On or Off.

Do It Yourself

Disable the Welcome screen (Windows XP Home/Pro only)

Require secure logon (Windows XP Pro and Windows 2000 only)

Create passwords for Windows accounts (XP Home/Pro and 2000 only)

Require a password for screensavers

Create a BIOS password

Change passwords for other hardware

Use strong passwords

Passwords to avoid

Web site passwords

How to remember all of your passwords

Prevent your Windows password from being lost or forgotten (XP Home/Pro only)

If you forget your Windows password (XP Home/Pro only)

If you forget your primary Windows password and don't have a password-reset disk (XP Home/Pro only)

Remove the "Password is About to Expire" notice (Windows XP Pro and Windows 2000 only)

Make folders private

5. Remove the checkmark from the Use the Welcome screen box (see Figure 16-1).

Figure 16-1

6. Click the Apply Option button.

Require Secure Logon (Windows XP Pro and Windows 2000 only)

To protect Windows from intruders, you can configure Windows so that it requires the Control, Alt, and Delete keys to be pressed simultaneously before a password can be entered.

For Windows XP Professional Edition

1. Click the Start button in the lower-left corner of Windows.

2. Click the Control Panel. (If you don't see this option, then your Start menu is in classic mode. In that case, click Settings, and then select the Control Panel.)

3. If the Control Panel is in category view, click the User Accounts category. If the Control Panel is in classic view, simply double-click the User Accounts icon.

4. A window opens. Click the Advanced tab.

5. Under the Secure Logon heading, put a checkmark in the Require users to press Ctrl+Alt+Delete box.

6. Click Apply.

7. Click OK.

Note

To use this feature, your Windows XP account must have administrative privileges and your computer must be part of a network domain (usually domains are found in offices or other business settings).

For Windows 2000

1. Click the Start button in the lower-left corner of Windows.

2. Click Settings.

3. Click the Control Panel.

4. Double-click the Users and Passwords icon.

5. Click the Advanced tab.

6. Under the Secure Boot Settings heading, put a checkmark in the Require users to press Ctrl+Alt+Delete box before logging on.

7. Click Apply.

8. Click OK.

Create Passwords for Windows Accounts (XP Home/Pro and 2000 only)

A key component in preventing intruders from accessing your Windows account is to protect it with a password. If you have not configured Windows to require a password, follow these steps.

Note

This information is not valid for older, outdated versions of Windows (such as 98) because they lack adequate security features.

For Windows XP Home Edition

1. Click the Start button in the lower-left corner of Windows.

2. Click the Control Panel. (If you don't see this option, then your Start menu is in classic mode. In that case, click Settings, and then select the Control Panel.)

3. If the Control Panel is in category view, click the User Accounts category. If the Control Panel is in classic view, simply double-click the User Accounts icon.

4. A window opens. Click on Change an Account.

5. Select the account you want to change.

6. Click on Create a Password.

7. Type a password of your choosing. Do not choose a word that can be guessed easily. For more information on creating passwords that are difficult to crack, refer to the "Use Strong Passwords" fix in this chapter.

8. Repeat this procedure for each Windows account. Give each user a separate, unique password.

For Windows XP Professional Edition and Windows 2000

1. Right-click the My Computer icon on your desktop. If this icon is not available, then click the Start button in the lower-left corner of Windows and right-click My Computer. If you can't find the My Computer icon anywhere, do the following:

   a. Right-click in the empty space on your desktop.

   b. Select Properties.

   c. A window opens. Click the Desktop tab.

   d. Near the bottom of the window, click the Customize Desktop button.

   e. Another window opens. On the General tab, beneath the words Desktop Icons, place a checkmark in the My Computer box.

   f. Click OK.

   g. You are returned to the previous screen. Click Apply.

   h. Click OK.

   i. The My Computer icon appears on your desktop. Right-click it.

2. Select Manage.

3. A window opens. In the left window pane, double-click the Local Users and Groups icon.

4. Below it, double-click the Users icon.

5. Right-click the account you want to change.

6. Select Set Password (see Figure 16-2).

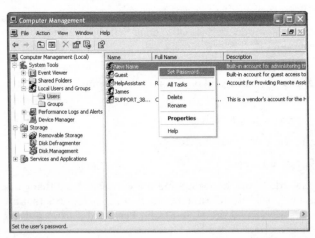

Figure 16-2

7. A window opens, into which you should type a new, strong password for the account.

Require a Password for Screensavers

If you use screensavers, you can enable a feature in Windows that will require
a password to be entered whenever the computer is awoken from its screensaver
"nap." This helps to protect your computer from being accessed by
unauthorized people.

1. Right-click in the empty space on your desktop.

2. Select Properties.

3. Click the Screen Saver tab.

4. For Windows 98, ME, and Windows 2000, put a checkmark in the
   Password Protected box. For Windows XP Home Edition, put a
   checkmark in the On resume, display Welcome screen box (see
   Figure 16-3). For Windows XP Professional Edition, put a checkmark
   in the On resume, password protect box.

Figure 16-3

5. Click Apply.

6. Click OK.

Create a BIOS Password

The motherboard is the device that acts like the nervous system for your
computer; it controls the signals and information that are distributed to your
various hardware devices. In the same way that a human nervous system is
regulated by a brain, the motherboard is regulated by a digital brain known as
the BIOS (which means Basic Input Output System). By changing the settings
in the BIOS, you can alter or enhance your computer's performance and create
a password that will prevent unauthorized people from tinkering with your
computer's hardware settings and booting your computer.

Note
When properly enabled, a BIOS password is required shortly after your computer
starts. If the password is not entered correctly, the computer refuses to do anything
and does not load Windows.

1. Most motherboards require you to press a special key on the
   keyboard to access the BIOS. On some computers, this key is one of
   the "F" keys (like F5 or F12) or the Delete key. To determine which
   key you need to press, consult the owner's manual for your computer.
   If you don't have a manual, then pay close attention to your monitor
   when the computer starts up. Usually a message will say "To enter
   BIOS press [*name of key*]."

2. When you have determined how to enter the BIOS, press the special
   key within a few seconds of starting the computer.

3. If nothing happens, and if Windows proceeds to load, then restart the
   computer and try again. This time try pressing the special key sooner
   or try pressing it a few times in a row to make sure the computer
   properly recognizes it.

4. After entering the BIOS, read the onscreen instructions for moving
   back and forth between the different screens and settings.

5. Look for an option labeled Set User Password or Set Supervisor
   Password (or something similar), and select it.

6. Enter a new password. For more information on creating passwords
   that are difficult to crack, refer to the fix "Use Strong Passwords" in
   this chapter.

7. Look for the Password Settings option (or something similar). If this
   option isn't available, then go to the next step. If this option exists,
   then select it and make sure that the password is set to *always* turn on
   each time the computer starts.

8. Before exiting the BIOS, be sure to select the Save Options and Exit
   option. That way, your changes will take effect.

Change Passwords for Other Hardware

Most devices used for networking computers — such as routers — have
password-protection features to prevent them from being hijacked by a hacker.
Generally, these devices are manufactured with a default password of "admin,"
which you should change. To learn how to access the password-protection features of your hardware, please consult its manual. For tips on creating strong
passwords that are difficult for criminals to crack, be sure to read the next fix.

Use Strong Passwords

To keep Internet intruders from breaking into your computer, you must create
strong passwords that are nearly impossible to crack. To explain why, let's use a
superhero metaphor. If your neighborhood is under attack by an evil, 50-foot-
tall robot that shoots lasers from its eyes, who would you rather call to defend

your neighborhood and battle the metallic menace: Robin (the teenage sidekick of Batman) or the Incredible Hulk? Sure, Robin may be swift and clever, and he has a nifty utility belt, but he just can't match the raw power of the mean, green, fighting machine known as the Hulk. When you create passwords for Windows or for e-commerce Web sites, be sure to "Hulkify" those passwords by making them strong.

- If you have a simple one-word password such as "computer," a high-tech thief could crack it in mere minutes.

- If you make the password more robust by adding numbers — as in computer33 — it might take the thief an extra 10 minutes to crack it.

- If your password is even more complex — as in comPut3r55@$ — the thief would have to work around the clock for days on end before he could come close to cracking it.

- Your password should have a *minimum* of six digits, with at least *three* of the following: lowercase letters, uppercase letters, numbers, and special characters.

- The easiest way to create a strong password is to develop a *passphrase*, which is a sentence you can easily remember. Use the first letter of each word in the passphrase to create a password. For example, the passphrase "Honk if you like computer geeks" becomes the password hiylcg. To make it even stronger, use a combination of uppercase and lowercase letters, numbers, and special characters that look like actual letters. For example, hiylcg can be changed into h1yLc&.

- For even stronger protection, change your passwords every six months.

Passwords to Avoid

Because many people have a difficult time remembering their passwords, they often use names or words that are near and dear to them — such as a pet's name. Although such passwords are easy to remember, they also are easy for a criminal to crack. Never use passwords containing:

- Nicknames for you or your family members

- A pet's name

- Your mother's maiden name

- The street number or street name of your current or former residences.

- Your relatives' names

- Sequential numbers (such as 1,2,3,4 or 6,7,8,9)

- Common words (such as the word "password" or "the")

- Words directly related to your occupation (if you are a doctor, don't use "doctor")

Web Site Passwords

If you use online banking or shop at e-merchants' Web sites, then you know that you are routinely asked to create usernames and passwords for those sites to prevent unauthorized people from accessing your online accounts. For convenience, the average person creates one memorable password and uses it for all the Web sites she visits. This is a serious mistake that can lead to identity theft. Think of it this way: using a single password is like having a single key that unlocks all of the doors to your house, all of your cars, your fire safe, your safe-deposit box at the bank, and more. If a criminal finds that one key, he can steal all of your belongings. To ensure maximum privacy and protection when surfing the Internet, use a separate, unique password for each Web site.

How to Remember All of Your Passwords

- Hand-write your usernames and passwords on a sheet of paper and store it in your personal fire safe at your home or office. Do not type this list on your computer because you must avoid leaving any traces of passwords on your hard drive (just in case your computer is stolen or hacked into).

- Use "vault" software. These programs act like a digital vault in which you can store, encrypt, and protect all of your passwords and usernames. That way, you have to remember only one password to access all of them.

Prevent Your Windows Password from Being Lost or Forgotten (XP Home/Pro only)

If you lose or forget your Windows XP password, you will be locked out of your computer. Prevent this by creating a "password-reset disk."

Note
This requires a floppy drive.

1. Locate a floppy disk that is blank and has been properly formatted.

2. Click the Start button in the lower-left corner of Windows.

3. Click the Control Panel. (If you don't see this option, then your Start menu is in classic mode. In that case, click Settings, and then select the Control Panel.)

4. If the Control Panel is in category view, click the User Accounts category. If the Control Panel is in classic view, simply double-click the User Accounts icon.

5. A window opens. If your Windows account has administrative privileges, then look for the Pick an Account to Change heading. Below it, click the name of your account. If your Windows account has limited privileges, then proceed to the next step.

6. In the upper-left corner, below the Related Tasks heading, click Prevent a forgotten password (see Figure 16-4).

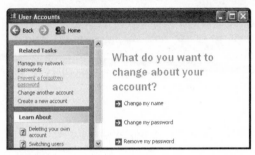

Figure 16-4

7. The Forgotten Password Wizard begins. Click Next.

8. Put your floppy disk into the disk drive.

9. Click Next.

10. In the Current User Account Password box, type your current password.

11. Click Next. This begins the creation of the password-reset disk.

12. When the process is finished, the progress bar indicates it is 100% complete. Click Next.

13. Click Finish.

14. Take the password-reset disk out of the disk drive and label it "Windows XP Password Reset Disk."

15. Store the disk in your home fire safe or in a safe-deposit box at your bank. Do not leave it lying around your home or office because if a criminal finds it, he can use it to access your computer.

If You Forget Your Windows Password (XP Home/Pro only)

Note
This requires a password-reset disk (as described in the previous fix).

1. Locate your password-reset disk.

2. Turn on your computer.

3. After Windows XP loads, you will see the Windows login screen. Click your username.

4. A box appears saying Type Your Password. Click the space where you would normally type your password, but don't type any words. Press the Enter key on your keyboard.

5. A message appears saying Did You Forget Your Password? To view your password hint, click the button with the question mark on it.

6. If, after reading the password hint, you still cannot remember your password, then click the words Use Your Password-Reset Disk. This launches the Password Reset Wizard.

7. Click Next.

8. Insert your password-reset disk into the floppy-disk drive.

9. Click Next.

10. In the Type a New Password box, enter a new password.

11. In the Type the Password Again to Confirm box, enter your new password a second time.

12. In the Type a New Password Hint box, type a few words that will help you to remember what your password is.

13. Click Next.

14. Click Finish.

15. You are taken back to the Windows XP login screen, where you should type your new password into the Type Your Password box.

16. Press the Enter key on your keyboard or click the button with the green arrow on it.

Note
After completing the Password Reset Wizard, your password-reset disk is automatically updated with your new password.

If You Forget Your Primary Windows Password and Don't Have a Password-Reset Disk (XP Home/Pro only)

Note
This tip doesn't apply if you have forgotten the passwords to all of your Windows XP user accounts or if your Windows XP computer is part of a workgroup or a domain (usually domains are found in offices or other business settings).

It's a Fact
You cannot use a password-reset disk on another computer — even if both computers have the same usernames and passwords.

Warning

If you use Windows XP Professional Edition, creating a new Windows password prevents you from accessing your previously encrypted files and e-mail as well as your Internet passwords.

1. Turn on your computer.

2. You will see the Windows Log-In screen. If you have a secondary or alternate Windows XP account with administrative privileges, click the name of that account and enter its password.

3. After Windows loads, click the Start button in the lower-left corner.

4. Click Run.

5. In the blank, type the words **control userpasswords2** (see Figure 16-5).

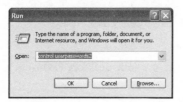

Figure 16-5

6. Click OK.

7. Click the name of the account for which you cannot remember the password.

8. Click the words Reset Password.

9. In the New Password box, type a new password.

10. In the Confirm New Password box, type your new password a second time.

11. Click OK.

12. Log out of Windows.

Now you should be able to log on to Windows with the new password and its corresponding username.

Remove the "Password Is About to Expire" Notice (Windows XP Pro and Windows 2000 only)

Every time you log on to Windows, do you get a message indicating your password is going to expire? You can tweak Windows so that your password never expires.

1. Right-click the My Computer icon on your desktop. If this icon is not available, then click the Start button in the lower-left corner of Windows and right-click My Computer. If you can't find the My Computer icon anywhere, do the following:

    a. Right-click in the empty space on your desktop.

    b. Select Properties.

    c. A window opens. Click the Desktop tab.

    d. Near the bottom of the window, click the Customize Desktop button.

    e. Another window opens. On the General tab, beneath the words Desktop Icons, place a checkmark in the My Computer box.

    f. Click OK.

    g. You are returned to the previous screen. Click Apply.

    h. Click OK.

    i. The My Computer icon appears on your desktop. Right-click it.

2. Select Manage.

3. Double-click the Local Users and Groups icon.

4. Double-click the Users icon.

5. In the right window pane, right-click the name of the account you want to change.

6. Select Properties (see Figure 16-6).

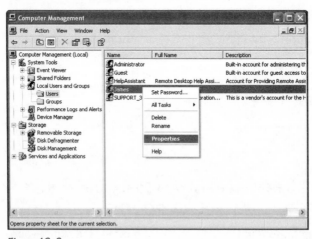

Figure 16-6

7. A window opens. Under the General tab, put a checkmark in the Password never expires box (see Figure 16-7).

Figure 16-7

8. Click Apply.

9. Click OK.

Make Folders Private

Do you share a computer with your family members or with your colleagues at the office? Do those users have their own Windows accounts? If so, it is possible for them to use their accounts to view your files and folders. To guard your data and prevent prying eyes, make your folders private.

For Windows XP Home Edition

1. Right-click the folder you want to make private.

2. Select Properties.

3. Click the Sharing tab.

4. Under the Local Sharing and Security heading, put a checkmark in the Make this folder private box (see Figure 16-8). If this option is grayed out, then the folder is already private.

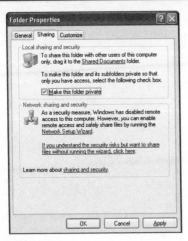

Figure 16-8

5. Click Apply.

6. Click OK.

For Windows XP Professional Edition and Windows 2000

1. Right-click the folder you want to make private.

2. Select Sharing and Security.

3. Click the Sharing tab.

4. Click the button labeled Do not share this folder (see Figure 16-9).

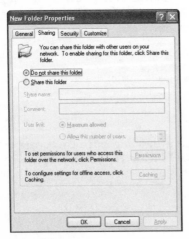

Figure 16-9

5. Click Apply.

6. Click OK.

For Windows 98 and ME

In these older versions of Windows, a very rudimentary way of sheltering your private files and folders is to make them invisible. This technique will not stop high-tech crooks from uncovering your data, but it will protect your critical information from being accidentally deleted by your children or by other people who use your computer.

1. Right-click the file or folder you want to hide.

2. Select Properties.

3. Put a checkmark in the Hidden box (see Figure 16-10).

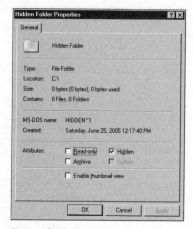

Figure 16-10

4. Click Apply.

5. Click Close.

6. The next time you try to access that file or folder, it will be invisible.

7. To access your hidden file, double-click the My Computer icon on your desktop.

8. Click the View drop-down menu.

9. Select Folder Options.

10. Click the View tab.

11. Click the button labeled Show all files (see Figure 16-11).

It's a Fact

If you use the System Restore feature of Windows XP, some passwords may not be restored, such as Windows passwords and their corresponding hints, along with passwords and hints for Internet Explorer. However, some passwords are restored, including passwords for instant-messaging programs and other software.

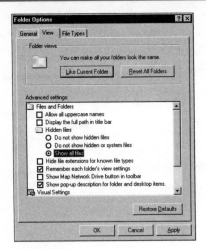

Figure 16-11

12. Click Apply.

13. Click OK.

14. Now you can return to the file or folder and view or access it normally.

15. To re-hide the file or folder, return to the View tab, but this time click the button labeled Do not show hidden or system files (see Figure 16-12).

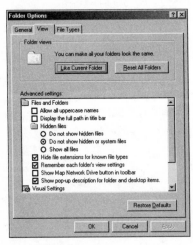

Figure 16-12

FYI

If you are desperate to recover a password and all else fails, you can purchase password-recovery software that might be able to retrieve your lost password. To find such a program, search for the phrase "password recovery software" on a popular Internet search engine such as Yahoo, MSN, or Google.

FYI

If your password is rejected by a program or a Web site, you might have accidentally pressed the Caps Lock key on your keyboard. Press it again, and then re-enter your password.

It's a Fact

One of the best ways to keep your passwords safe from criminals is to keep them a secret! Don't share them with anyone.

17

DATA DELETION

H ave you ever wondered what really happens to a file
when you delete it? If you are like most
people, you probably assume that when a file is
deleted, it is gone for good, right? Wrong.

Data Afterlife

- When a file is deleted in Windows, it is sent to the
  Recycle Bin (the icon on your desktop that looks
  like a garbage can). At this point, the file has not
  actually disappeared. Instead, it is sitting in a type
  of suspended animation inside the Recycle Bin, just
  waiting to be discarded. Changes cannot be made to
  a file in the Recycle Bin, nor can the file be opened
  or viewed.

- If you change your mind and decide you want to
  keep the file, you can open the Recycle Bin,
  right-click the file, and choose to restore it. The file
  vanishes from the Recycle Bin and reappears in its
  original location.

- If you decide that you want to rid yourself of that
  file, you can choose to empty the Recycle Bin.

What Happens When the Recycle Bin Is Emptied?

- In a sense, all of its files are flushed down the
  digital drain. But be careful. If those files contain
  sensitive information, they can come back to
  bite you.

- A file is like a road-sign that tells Windows where to
  locate some data on your hard drive. When you
  delete a file and empty it from the Recycle Bin, you
  are destroying only the road-sign — not the actual
  data. That means the data is just sitting in limbo on
  your hard drive until it is overwritten by new data.

Do It Yourself

Data afterlife

What happens when
the Recycle Bin is
emptied?

Delete data once and
for all

Wiping software

How to safely sell or
donate your
computer

How to wipe your
computer

Properly disposing of
a hard drive

Properly disposing of
CDs, DVDs, floppy
disks, and Zip disks

- Your deleted data can be recovered by someone who has the appropriate software and computer smarts. That's good news for you if you accidentally deleted the Great American Novel you are writing, but it is bad news if your computer is hacked into, if you donate your computer to a charity, or if you sell it on eBay.

- If your computer data is not properly destroyed, it could be recovered and used by criminals to commit identity theft.

Delete Data Once and for All

- The only safe way to get rid of your files is to wipe them from existence — literally. Special software exists that can *wipe* data (also known as *shredding*), which will make the files almost impossible to recover.

- During the wiping process, your old files are overwritten numerous times by new, random data. Think of it like painting the same wall in your house over and over with a different color each time.

Wiping Software

You can buy professional wiping programs from retail stores or e-merchants, or you can download free ones from the Internet. The choice depends on how much (or little) money you are willing to spend and how serious you are about keeping your deleted data safe from prying eyes. Some programs give a better, more secure wipe, whereas others barely make the grade. Here are some options (in no particular order):

- File Shredder (www.stompsoft.com)

- BCWipe (www.jetico.com)

- Steganos Security Suite (www.steganos.com)

How to Safely Sell or Donate Your Computer

- Copy your important files from your old computer to your new one. This can be done by burning the files to a data-backup device. Do not cut and paste your files from your old computer to your new one because you want to leave the original versions of your data intact so you can wipe them.

- To prevent the next owner of your computer from retrieving your deleted files, wipe all of your private data on the hard drive and all rewriteable disks (floppies, Zip disks, CD/DVDs, and so on).

How to Wipe Your Computer

To wipe an entire hard drive, you will need to purchase special drive-wiping software that will erase every trace of data from the drive.

Note
Use this option only if you are planning to reinstall Windows on the computer prior to selling it. Otherwise, the computer will not have an operating system and will be unusable.

Here are some popular drive-wiping programs (in no particular order):

- WipeDrive (`www.whitecanyon.com`)
- BCWipe (`www.jetico.com`)
- EraserDisk (`www.micro2000.co.uk/products/eraserdisk/eraserdisk.htm`)
- Acronis Drive Cleanser (`www.acronis.com/enterprise/products/drivecleanser`)
- DriveScrubber (`www.iolo.com`)

Note
If you are planning to throw away your computer, you should physically destroy your hard drive. Please see the following fix, "Properly Disposing of a Hard Drive."

Note
If you are planning to sell or donate your computer, you should reinstall Windows after the wiping is complete.

1. Locate the CD-ROM containing your Windows operating system. Sometimes this disc is labeled Windows Recovery CD.

2. Turn on the computer, and then immediately insert the disc into your CD drive.

3. The computer should recognize the CD and begin the process of installing Windows.

4. Follow the onscreen instructions.

Properly Disposing of a Hard Drive

Let's say your hard drive crashed. Kaput. Fried. Deep-sixed. Dead. What do you do with it? Maybe you take it to a computer recycling center or just toss it in the trash. Or maybe you use it as a paperweight. Or maybe you place it on your coffee table and use it as a shiny, ultra-modern coaster for drinks. No matter what you decide, keep in mind that even though your hard drive no longer works, your data may still be alive and kicking.

When disposing of a hard drive, the best way to ensure that your data cannot be recovered by a thief is to physically damage the drive. So grab a hammer, mallet, or a blunt tool and start pounding away. Not only will it make your data nearly impossible to recover, but it's also a great stress reliever.

Properly Disposing of CDs, DVDs, Floppy Disks, and Zip Disks

Just like a hard drive, a CD or DVD containing your data must be destroyed before being thrown away. Failure to do so could result in your data being stolen by anyone who has the time (and a good set of nose-plugs) to rummage through your garbage. There are two ways to dispose of a CD/DVD properly:

Use a special CD/DVD shredding device: Similar in appearance to a paper shredder, this device is specially designed to shred your discs into hundreds of little pieces.

Use scissors to cut the discs: A simple, old-fashioned way to destroy CDs or DVDs is to cut them into several pieces by using a standard pair of scissors.

For Zip disks and cassettes: Treat them like a hard drive and destroy them with a hammer or similar tool.

It's a Fact

The majority of previously owned computers found in pawn shops, sold on Web sites such as eBay, or donated to charity contain sensitive data that has not been properly deleted. Before you get rid of your computer, make sure you wipe all traces of yourself from it.

FYI

Old computers shouldn't be tossed in the garbage—even if they're broken—because they can poison the environment. Some computer parts contain toxic materials that can leak into the ground and contaminate water supplies. Always take old hardware to a computer-recycling center or a hazardous-waste dump.

18

DATA
ENCRYPTION

So you've heeded the advice in this book, followed all of the steps, and battened down the hatches in your computer. Finally you can sit back, relax, sip a frosty beverage, and thumb your nose at digital threats and Internet intruders. But as you enjoy that tasty drink, consider this question: If a criminal steals or hacks into your computer, would he be able to view your private data? If you haven't encrypted your files, the answer is Yes.

Deadbolt Your Data

If you have ever seen a spy movie, you know that encryption is the process of transforming your data into a secret code that can be viewed only by people with the correct password. With the crime of identity theft growing worse each year, encryption has become a vital part of protecting yourself from high-tech hoodlums.

Note

If your computer has Windows XP Professional Edition or Windows 2000, you can simply use its built-in encryption features. However, if your computer runs Windows 95, 98, ME, or XP Home Edition, then you need to install encryption software.

Encryption Software

A variety of software manufacturers have encryption programs that you can download from the Internet. Some may take a bite out of your wallet, but others will set you back only a few bucks. Your best bet is to select one that provides reliable technical support, which is crucial if you ever encrypt your data and then can't unlock it.

Do It Yourself

Deadbolt your data

Encryption software

Windows encryption (XP Pro and Windows 2000 only)

Encrypt a file

Encrypt a folder

Give encryption permission (Windows XP Pro only)

Encryption tips (Windows XP Pro and Windows 2000 only)

Encrypt the Temp folder

Encrypt Offline Files (Windows XP Pro only)

Steganography

- WinZip (www.winzip.com)
- PGP Corporation (www.pgp.com)
- CryptoForge (www.cryptoforge.com)
- BestCrypt (www.jetico.com)
- DriveCrypt (www.securstar.com)
- Turbocrypt (www.pmc-ciphers.com)
- Steganos Safe 8 (www.steganos.com)
- Cryptainer (www.cypherix.com)
- Secure IT (www.cypherix.com)

Windows Encryption (XP Pro and Windows 2000 only)

Using the built-in, on-the-fly encryption features of Windows XP Professional Edition and Windows 2000 is just as easy as working with normal, everyday files.

Note
This encryption requires the NTFS file system.

Encrypt a File
1. Right-click the file you want to encrypt.
2. Select Properties.
3. Under the General tab, click the Advanced button.
4. A window opens. At the bottom of it, put a checkmark in the Encrypt contents to secure data box (see Figure 18-1). If this option is grayed out, then Windows encryption is not available. You will need to install a separate encryption program.

Figure 18-1

5. Click OK.

6. Click Apply.

7. A message appears asking if you want to encrypt just the file or encrypt it *and* the folder it is stored in (see Figure 18-2). If the file is one that you plan to make changes to, then choose to encrypt it *and* its folder. This ensures that the file remains encrypted.

Figure 18-2

8. Once you have made your choice, click OK.

9. In Windows XP Professional Edition, you will notice that the name of the file has green letters instead of the usual black letters. This indicates your file is properly encrypted (see Figure 18-3).

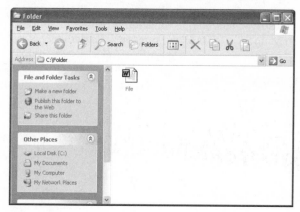

Figure 18-3

Encrypt a Folder

1. Right-click the folder you want to encrypt.

2. Select Properties.

3. Under the General tab, click Advanced.

4. A window opens. At the bottom of it, put a checkmark in the Encrypt contents to secure data box (see Figure 18-4). If this option is grayed out, then Windows encryption is not available. You will need to install a separate encryption program.

Figure 18-4

5. Click OK.

6. Click Apply.

7. A message appears asking you if you want to encrypt just the folder or encrypt it *and* all of the other folders inside of it (as well as the files in those other folders; see Figure 18-5). If you are encrypting an important folder such as My Documents, you should choose to encrypt the folder *and* its subfolders so that all of your sensitive documents are protected.

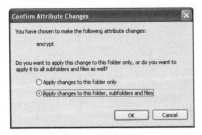

Figure 18-5

8. Once you have made your selection, click OK.

9. In Windows XP Professional Edition, you will notice that the name of the folder has green letters instead of the usual black letters (see Figure 18-6). This indicates your folder is properly encrypted.

Note
Any files you add to an encrypted folder are automatically encrypted.

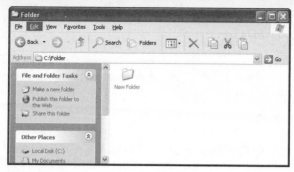

Figure 18-6

Give Encryption Permission (Windows XP Pro only)

If you would like to allow other accounts on your computer to view your encrypted files, you need to grant them special permission. For example, if you, your spouse, and each of your children have separate Windows accounts, you can permit your spouse but not your children to view your encrypted data.

1. Right-click the encrypted file or folder.

2. Select Properties.

3. Click the Advanced button.

4. Click the Details button.

5. A window opens. In the center of it, click the Add button.

6. Another window opens. Select the name of the account you want to give permission to, and then click OK (see Figure 18-7).

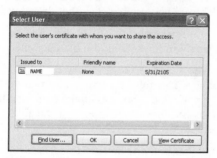

Figure 18-7

7. You are returned to the previous window. Click OK.

Encryption Tips (Windows XP Pro and Windows 2000 only)

In addition to encrypting private data such as financial statements, you can increase your protection against Internet intruders by encrypting the Temp folder and Offline Files.

Encrypt the Temp Folder

1. Double-click the My Computer icon on your desktop. If this icon is not available, then click the Start button in the lower-left corner of Windows and click My Computer. If you can't find the My Computer icon anywhere, do the following:

   a. Right-click in the empty space on your desktop.

   b. Select Properties.

   c. A window opens. Click the Desktop tab.

   d. Near the bottom of the window, click the Customize Desktop button.

   e. Another window opens. On the General tab, beneath the words Desktop Icons, place a checkmark in the My Computer box.

   f. Click OK.

   g. You are returned to the previous screen. Click Apply.

   h. Click OK.

   i. The My Computer icon appears on your desktop. Right-click it.

2. Double-click the icon for your C: drive (unless you installed Windows in a different location, in which case you double-click that drive letter).

3. If you are using Windows XP Professional Edition, double-click the Windows folder. If you are using Windows 2000, double-click the WINNT folder.

4. You might see a warning that says This folder contains files that keep your system working properly; you should not modify its contents. If so, click the words below it that say Show the contents of this folder. Otherwise, proceed to the next step.

5. Scroll through the folders until you find one labeled Temp (see Figure 18-8). Right-click it.

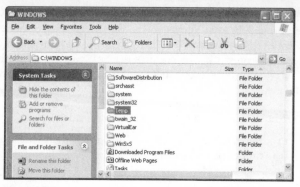

Figure 18-8

6. Select Properties.

7. Under the General tab, click the Advanced button.

8. A window opens. At the bottom of it, put a checkmark in the Encrypt contents to secure data box. If this option is grayed out, then Windows encryption is not available. You will need to install a separate encryption program.

9. Click OK.

10. Click Apply.

11. A message appears asking you if you want to encrypt just the folder or encrypt it and all of the other folders inside of it (as well as the files in those other folders). See Figure 18-9. Choose to encrypt the folder *and* its subfolders.

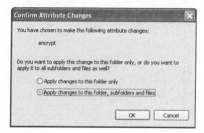

Figure 18-9

12. Click OK.

Encrypt Offline Files (Windows XP Pro only)

The Offline Files option in Windows allows you to save Web pages or network folders onto your computer so you can view them after you have disconnected from the Internet or a local network. For security reasons, you should avoid Offline Files. However, if you want to use them, you can enhance your security by encrypting them.

1. Click the Start button in the lower-left corner of Windows.

2. Click the Control Panel. (If you don't see this option, then your Start menu is in classic mode. In that case, click Settings, and then select the Control Panel.)

3. If the Control Panel is in category view, click the Appearance and Themes category, and then click the Folder Options icon. If the Control Panel is in classic view, simply double-click the Folder Options icon.

4. A window opens. Click the Offline Files tab.

5. If you want to use offline files but haven't yet enabled this feature, then click Enable offline files.

6. Put a checkmark in the Encrypt offline files to secure data box (see Figure 18-10).

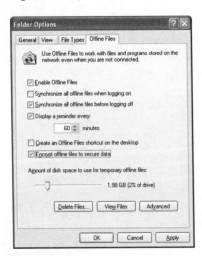

Figure 18-10

7. Click OK.

Steganography

Another method of securing data is to use *steganography* software, which allows you to hide your files in the empty space of digital photos, digital music, and more. Those pictures or songs can be viewed or played normally, and no one but you will ever know there is more than meets the eye. Typically, steganography is used to supplement encryption rather than replace it, but it can be a great alternative if you cannot or do not use encryption. This software is not included with Windows, so you will need to install it manually. Here are some popular steganography programs (in no particular order):

- Steganos Security Suite (`www.steganos.com`)

- iStegano (`www.intrancesoftworks.com`) has encryption and steganography

- Steganography (`www.securekit.com`)

19

DATA BACKUP

Financial documents, MP3 music files, precious digital photos of your pet poodle dressed in a cowboy outfit—these are some examples of the irreplaceable data stored in your computer. Chances are, if this data were to vanish suddenly, your whole life would be negatively affected. Undoubtedly your screams of frustration would be heard from miles away, and your head would be full of bald spots from tearing out your hair. Save time, headaches, and your hairline—back up your computer!

Reasons to Back Up Your Computer Data

Dead hard drive: The files on your computer are stored on a hard drive, which is basically a box containing a metal platter that rotates at high speeds. If segments of the hard drive become corrupt or damaged, the data stored on the drive cannot be read properly (just like a music CD that skips if it has too many scratches). Also, hard drives are just like any other electronic gadget—they are designed by secret cabals of electronic manufacturers that have conspired to create devices that last only for short periods of time so consumers must constantly buy new ones. Okay, so this conspiracy theory is just a joke, but hard drive failure is not. It can happen without warning for no apparent reason.

Killer virus: Some computer viruses and other digital threats lurking on the Internet have the capability to destroy certain types of files on your computer.

Power surge: A fluctuation in your power line or an electrical storm can cause a sudden burst of electricity to race into your computer and fry your hard drive and other computer parts.

Do It Yourself

Reasons to back up your computer data

When to back up your computer data

Backup devices

External hard drive

Internal hard drive

Recordable or rewriteable CD/DVD burners

RAID your computer

How to copy data to a backup device

Buy burning software from a store

Use Windows XP

Backup options

Manually back up your important files

Create a disc image

Where to store backed-up data

Theft: Computers, especially laptops, are a big target for thieves. Having your computer stolen is a double whammy because not only do you lose your data, but the thief has complete access to it and can use it to commit identity theft. For more information about protecting your identity, see Chapter 22.

Fire and natural disasters: Fires, hurricanes, tornadoes, floods, and other weather phenomena can damage or destroy your computer along with any backed-up data that you have lying around your home or office. Consider off-site data storage, which is examined later in this chapter.

Children: Whether your children are a few years old or a few decades old, the chances are good that at some point they will use your computer (and probably leave crumbs all over your keyboard!). Whether they mean to or not, your kids could delete a particular document or file that has great importance to you. Prevent this by backing up your data, protecting your Windows account with a password, and setting up separate accounts for each of your family members.

When to Back Up Your Data

The frequency of your backup depends on how often you create new data that you consider to be critical or irreplaceable.

For home: If you create important data on a regular basis, back up your entire hard drive weekly or bi-weekly and make individual copies of your most important files on a daily basis (which can be done with a USB thumbdrive).

For offices: Because most companies create new, critical data every day, a complete backup of all files on all computers should be performed daily.

Backup Devices

There's no right or wrong kind of backup device to use; each has benefits and drawbacks. Base your decision on what you feel most comfortable using and what your checking account says you can afford.

External Hard Drive

In a nutshell, this device is a typical computer hard drive housed in a rugged shell to protect it from drops, shocks, and spills. It connects to your computer via USB or FireWire cables.

Benefits: Holds a massive amount of data (likely more than you need), is portable, and can be used with multiple computers in the same home or office.

Drawbacks: Bulky, somewhat expensive, and is prone to unexpected crashes or failures just like any type of hard drive.

Internal Hard Drive

Benefits: Usually less expensive than external versions, does not take up space on your desk, and holds large amounts of data.

Drawbacks: Must be installed by someone who is familiar with opening a computer and upgrading its parts; has the same potential for crashes or failures like any hard drive.

Recordable or Rewriteable CD/DVD Burners

Available in external and internal versions, these devices allow you to copy data onto write-once discs or rewriteable discs. There are many types of burners and discs available, which often can be confusing. Here is a quick guideline:

CD-R: The original recordable CD format. Stores 650 to 700 megabytes of data on a single, write-once disc (which means the data is permanently burned to the disc).

CD-RW: Has the same capacity as CD-R discs, but can be erased and reused hundreds or even thousands of times.

DVD-R: Stores up to 4.7 gigabytes of data on DVD discs that are identical in size to the DVD movies you watch at home. Most of these devices are backward compatible with CD-R and CD-RW, meaning they can read and write data from the aforementioned CD discs.

DVD-RW: Has same storage capacity as DVD-R, but can be erased and reused hundreds or even thousands of times. These devices usually have backward compatibility with CD-R and CD-RW.

DVD+R: Here is where it gets tricky. Notice that this type of DVD has a "plus" sign (+) rather than a "minus" sign (-). The "plus" (+) discs cannot be used in "minus" (-) drives, and vice versa. Other than that, both formats have the same 4.7 gigabyte storage capacity.

DVD+RW: Same restriction about not mixing "plus" discs and "minus" discs, and has the same storage capacity as the other DVD formats. Can be erased and reused hundreds or even thousands of times.

Multi-format DVD burners: These devices bypass the war between the "plus" discs and the "minus" discs by allowing you to use any of the four kinds: -R, -RW, +R, or +RW. This is the best option because it gives you the most flexibility when purchasing discs.

Dual-layer DVD (DL): These discs store approximately 8.4 gigabytes of data, which is twice the capacity of a normal DVD disc. Most of these burners are backward compatible with the other DVD formats.

USB thumbdrives: These devices give you quick storage in a small package—about the size of a stick of gum. They are commonly available in capacities of 128 megabytes, 256 megabytes, 512 megabytes, or 1 gigabyte, and they plug into the USB ports on your computer (the same ports into which you plug a USB printer or a digital camera).

Tape drives: Used primarily by businesses, these devices store data on cassette tapes that have large capacities (generally several hundred gigabytes).

RAID Your Computer

If you are bold—the kind of person who likes a drink shaken, not stirred—you might consider a more complicated form of data backup that also gives a boost in computer performance: RAID (which stands for Redundant Array of Independent Discs). Quite a mouthful, huh? In simple terms, it means you have two identical hard drives inside your computer, each of which is a clone of the other (having the exact same operating system, programs, and files configured in the exact same way). Not only will a RAID allow you to use certain programs and files faster (especially video-editing software), but it also protects you from a hard-drive crash by allowing you to use the clone to continue operating your computer (and, mostly important, no data is lost). Creating a RAID requires a good understanding of computer basics and a motherboard inside your computer that is RAID capable. To see if your motherboard makes the grade—and for instructions on setting up a RAID—consult its owner's manual.

How to Copy Data to a Backup Device

You need special software that acts as a go-between to tell your computer what data to copy. Most backup devices come with some type of specialized software, so consult the owner's manuals and CD-ROMs for your computer or backup device. If you do not have such software, there are two choices.

Buy Burning Software from a Store

You might consider this option even if your backup device came with free burning software because more than likely that free software is a no-frills, stripped-down version that is barely adequate.

Use Windows XP

If you have Windows XP Home Edition or Professional Edition, you can use the basic CD/DVD burning feature built into it.

1. Right-click the file or folder you want to back up.

2. Select Copy.

3. Double-click the My Computer icon on your desktop. If this icon is not available, then click the Start button in the lower-left corner of

Windows and click My Computer. If you can't find the My Computer icon anywhere, do the following:

a. Right-click in the empty space on your desktop.

b. Select Properties.

c. A window opens. Click the Desktop tab.

d. Near the bottom of the window, click the Customize Desktop button.

e. Another window opens. On the General tab, beneath the words Desktop Icons, place a checkmark in the My Computer box.

f. Click OK.

g. You are returned to the previous screen. Click Apply.

h. Click OK.

i. The My Computer icon appears on your desktop. Right-click it.

4. Right-click the icon for your CD or DVD burner.

5. Select Paste.

6. You should see a balloon message that says You have files waiting to be written to the CD (see Figure 19-1). If so, click it. If this message doesn't appear, then double-click the icon for your CD or DVD burner.

Figure 19-1

7. In the upper-left corner of Windows, click the File drop-down menu.

8. Select Write These Files to CD.

9. The CD Writing Wizard launches. Follow the onscreen instructions to burn your data to disc.

Backup Options

The most common methods of backing up data are to do it manually or to create a disc image.

Manually Back Up Your Important Files

In this case, you back up only your documents, photos, music files, or any other data you consider irreplaceable. However, you do not back up Windows or your entire hard drive.

Benefits: The backup software that came with your computer or with your backup device is all you need, so you don't have to spend extra money. Often this method is more simple and quick.

Drawbacks: If your hard drive crashes, your data is safe but you face the unenviable task of reinstalling Windows, reinstalling all of the patches and security updates for Windows, and reinstalling all of your software.

Popular burning programs (in no particular order):

- Nero Burning ROM or Nero Express (www.nero.com)
- Roxio Easy Media Creator (www.roxio.com)
- NTI CD-Maker (www.ntius.com)

Create a Disc Image

By using special software, you can create an image of your hard drive, which is a fancy way of saying that you are backing up the entire contents of your hard drive—including Windows and all software.

Benefits: If your hard drive ever crashes and you lose data, all you have to do is load the disc image onto your computer, and you will be up and running as if nothing ever happened. This software can be used with almost any backup device (external/internal hard drives, CD/DVD burners, and so on).

Drawbacks: Usually disc-imaging software does not come with a backup device, so it must be purchased separately. Also, it can be slow as well as difficult to learn and use.

Popular disc-imaging programs (in no particular order):

- Norton Ghost (www.symantec.com)
- Turbo Backup (www.filestream.com)
- Acronis True Image (www.acronis.com)
- NTI Backup NOW (www.ntius.com)

Where to Store Backed-Up Data

How important is your data? To some people, their one-of-a-kind computer files—such as digital photos—are priceless. What about your files? How much are they worth to you? If you back up your computer and simply leave that data lying on your desk or stuffed in a bookshelf somewhere, you are gambling that nothing is going to happen to it. But what if someone burglarizes your home or office? Or what if you fall

FYI

The average lifespan of a hard drive is only three to six years. Back up your data now, before it's too late!

It's a Fact

To save your hard drive — and your irreplaceable data — from being obliterated by a lightning strike, unplug your computer during a thunder or lightning storm.

FYI

Surge protectors are essential to prevent your hardware and data from being damaged or destroyed by a power surge. (Sorry, but common household power-strips don't qualify as surge protectors.) An even better solution is an Uninterruptible Power Supply (also known as "battery backup") that protects against harmful dips in electricity called "brownouts" and, in the event of a blackout, gives you enough power to save your files and shut down your computer safely.

victim to a fire, flood, or natural disaster? Rather than leave your data out in the open, consider a better alternative.

Fire safe: Whether your data is backed up onto discs, hard drives, thumbdrives, or cassettes, you can store it in a fire safe. Although many of the standard fire safes found at popular stores are capable of withstanding water or extreme temperatures only for one or two hours, at least that buys you some time. Also, a fire safe provides a good measure of protection against burglars. When using a safe at home, place it in an inconspicuous area of the house and bolt it to the floor beams or to the wood studs in a wall (to prevent a thief from carrying away the safe and cracking it open later). As an extra measure of precaution, do not share the combination to your safe with people outside your immediate "circle of trust" (to quote the movie *Meet the Parents*). And no matter what, don't make the mistake of leaving the keys to your safe lying around your house where an intruder can find them. Then again, the same could be said for any spare keys for your house, car, and so on. A simple solution is a key lockbox that can be bolted to a wall.

Off-site storage: The best method of protecting your data is to store it in a highly secure off-site location, such as a safe-deposit box at a bank. That way, no matter what happens to your home or office, your data will survive. This option requires a monthly or yearly fee, but that amount is insignificant compared to the value of your data.

PART VI
PRIVACY PROTECTION

The Global Village

Many scholars and politicians have referred to our digitally connected world as a "global village." Thanks to the Internet, e-mail, instant messages, cell phones, and other amazing technologies, our planet is connected as never before. But there is a downside: We no longer enjoy the same privacy we once had. The development of new communication devices has led to an increase in high-tech crimes, spurring law-enforcement agencies to develop special cyber taskforces to deal with this growing problem. Unfortunately, it seems like the authorities are always one step behind those digital delinquents, so it is up to you to take action to restore some of that old-fashioned privacy.

20

SAFELY USE PUBLIC COMPUTERS

Be careful when using a public computer at a library, airport, copy shop, or Internet café. If you don't cover your tracks, whoever uses the computer after you might be able to see the sites you visited or uncover information about you.

Be Private in Public

You should take several actions to protect your privacy in a public setting.

> **Be careful what you type:** The possibility exists that a criminal could have installed a "keystroke logger" program on a public computer to record everything you type on the keyboard. To stay safe, avoid sites such as online banks or e-merchants that require you to type an account number, credit-card number, or password.

> **Disable AutoComplete:** If the public computer runs Windows, it may have the AutoComplete feature turned on. Disable it to prevent your passwords from being remembered. For more information, refer to Chapter 2.

> **Avoid automatic log-ins:** Many Web sites and programs allow you to save your username and password so you don't have to retype them every time you visit the site or run the program. Avoid these automatic log-ins to prevent someone from purposefully or accidentally logging on to your account.

> **Watch for wandering eyes:** An easy way for a thief to steal your passwords or other sensitive information requires no technology—all he has to

do is look over your shoulder while you type. Keep an eye out for these snoops.

Stay with the computer: If you are in the middle of an Internet session, don't walk away from the computer to talk to someone, to use the bathroom, and so on. If you need to stretch your legs, log out of all Web sites and programs and close any open folders or windows.

Log out properly: If you previously logged in to a Web site (such as Web-based e-mail), always click the words Log Out to safely close your session. Usually the log-out option is located in the top-left or -right of the Web page.

Erase your trail: When you have completely finished using a public computer, wipe away the tracks you may have left behind.

1. Open Internet Explorer.

2. Click the Tools drop-down menu.

3. Select Internet Options.

4. Click the General tab.

5. Under the Temporary Internet Files heading, click the Delete Cookies button (see Figure 20-1).

Figure 20-1

6. A window opens that says Delete All Cookies in the Temporary Internet Files Folder? Click OK.

7. Under the History heading, click the Clear History button.

8. A window opens that says Are You Sure You Want Windows to Delete Your History of Visited Web sites? Click Yes.

9. Click the Delete Files button.

10. Put a checkmark in the Delete all offline content box, and then click OK.

11. To exit the Internet Options, click OK.

21

PROTECT LAPTOPS

Smaller. Faster. Lighter. Modern computers have come a long way since their behemoth beginnings in the 1950s. But as they keep shrinking, keep in mind that the smaller they are, the easier they are to steal.

Lock Down Your Laptop

So far, all of the advice in this book has been applicable to desktop and laptop computers alike. But now we're going to switch gears and talk about specific things you should do to keep your laptop from falling into the wrong hands.

Create a BIOS password: The first line of defense is to create a password for your laptop's BIOS. That way, if a thief nabs your laptop, he or she won't be able to boot into Windows (at least not without great effort). For more information on BIOS passwords, refer to Chapter 16.

Create a Windows password: The second line of defense is to create a password for your Windows account. That way, even if a thief cracks your BIOS password, he faces yet another obstacle. For more information on Windows passwords, refer to Chapter 16.

Use strong passwords: By making your BIOS and Windows passwords complex, you make it nearly impossible for a thief to crack them. For more information on creating strong passwords, refer to Chapter 16.

Do It Yourself

Lock down your laptop

Back up your data: Thieves aren't the only hazards your laptop faces: It can be dropped down a flight of stairs, knocked into a bathtub, run over by a lawnmower, or countless other goofs that resemble the shenanigans of a television sitcom. Protect your irreplaceable data — back it up. For more information, refer to Chapter 19.

Encrypt your data: Although passwords will deter casual thieves, professional criminals might be able to circumvent them. The best way to keep your private data safe from prying eyes is to encrypt it. For more information on data encryption, refer to Chapter 18.

Don't use conspicuous cases: You can always spot laptop users — they're the ones carrying cases designed especially for laptops. Sure, those cases provide much needed storage and protection, but they also scream out "Hey, thieves! Over here! Check out the valuable piece of equipment in here!" Instead, consider using a standard, nondescript briefcase, backpack, or duffle bag that blends in with the crowd.

Be hands-on: The best way to keep your laptop from falling into the wrong hands is to keep it in your hands at all times. A laptop stored in overhead bins in an airplane is easy pickings for an experienced thief — as is a laptop sitting in the seat next to you on the subway or in a cab.

Keep your eyes peeled: If you have no choice but to store your laptop, keep it close by. Put it directly under your seat or in the overhead bin directly above you. And keep an eye on it (which means no naps!).

Write down the serial number: Just like TVs, DVD players, and other electronic equipment, every laptop has a unique serial number. Think of it like a digital fingerprint; no two are alike. Write down this number on a slip of paper and store it somewhere secure (like your fire safe). If your laptop is stolen, give the serial number to the police. Maybe, just maybe, they might track down your laptop at a local pawn shop.

Engrave your name: Having your name engraved on your laptop gives police another means of locating your stolen equipment.

Use tracking software: A few companies make special software you can install on your laptop to assist in recovering it in the event of theft. If the thief connects your laptop to an Internet connection, the software contacts you and gives you his approximate location, which you can pass along to the police. (But don't be foolish and try to go after the criminal yourself; the Charles Bronson tough-guy act may work in a Hollywood movie, but not in real life.) Here are some reputable laptop-tracking programs (in no particular order):

- ZTrace (www.ztrace.com)

- CyberAngel (www.sentryinc.com)

- Computrace (www.absolute.com)

22

IDENTITY THEFT

5-Minute Fixes

I n the movie *The Talented Mr. Ripley*, Matt Damon plays a character who bumps off a man and steals his identity. In real life, identity thieves don't have to resort to violence; we make it all too easy for them to find what they need with minimal effort. But don't despair; there are many things you can do to protect yourself from the Mr. Ripleys of the world.

Thwart Identity Thieves

Dumpsters, garbage cans, stolen wallets or purses, vulnerable computer networks — these are the playground of the identity thief. The average person does little to protect his or her sensitive information from evil-doers, which is why identity theft is one of the fastest-growing crimes in America. Although many financial institutions have identity-theft policies in place to protect their customers' accounts from being drained or being maxed out, it can take months or years to get everything straightened out — and in the meantime, your FICO credit score can take a serious beating. To avoid becoming a statistic, take charge of your identity. Be proactive.

> **Use unique passwords:** If you're like most Internet users, you probably have numerous accounts for online banking, Web mail, e-commerce, news sites, and more. And like most Web surfers, you probably use the same password for all of those sites. This is extremely risky because if a criminal discovers that password, he has unrestricted access to all of your accounts. To protect yourself, use a different, unique password for each site. If you have difficulty remembering all of the passwords, create a handwritten list and store it in your fire safe. Do not keep this list on your computer (unless you plan to encrypt it) because anyone who steals your computer will be able to hijack your accounts and seize your private information. An alternative is to store your passwords in a special "vault" program.

Do It Yourself

Thwart identity thieves

Surf anonymously

Guard your identity

If you are a victim of identity theft

Encrypt your computer data: Does your computer contain financial statements, credit-card numbers, business documents, names and addresses of friends and family, or other private information that would be a jackpot to an identity thief? The only way to protect your data and give yourself peace of mind is to encrypt your files by using special software. For more information, refer to Chapter 18.

Protect your privacy: Be careful about the private information you divulge on the Internet; you never know who might stumble across it. Stay away from online surveys that ask you about your income level, your shopping preferences, or how many people are in your household. When asked by Web sites to give your age, date of birth, home address, or e-mail address, give fake information (unless the site is for e-commerce, in which case you must be truthful to complete your purchase).

Guard your social security number: If a criminal gets his hands on your social security number, he could use it to have a copy of your social security card issued to him, which would enable him to sign up for new credit cards with your name on them that would be mailed to his home. Shortly thereafter, he would embark on a wild shopping spree, and your credit history would receive a black eye. To protect yourself, never list your social security number on your driver's license, never use it as your college ID, and never use it as a log-in for online banking or similar Web sites. As a rule of thumb, the less you publicize your social security number, the safer you are.

Avoid automatic log-ins: Some Web sites or programs allow you to save your user IDs and passwords so you don't have to re-enter them every time you visit those sites or run those programs. However, this can make it easy for a thief to access your accounts if he steals or hacks into your computer. Avoiding automatic log-ins may be an inconvenience, but it enhances your security.

Always log out: Before exiting an Internet account such as online banking or Web mail, always click the button or words Log Off or Log Out. This closes your session on that site and prevents someone from breaking into your account by clicking the Back button in your Web browser.

Avoid credit-card auto-save: Most e-commerce Web sites allow you to store credit-card numbers in their databases to make your future transactions quicker and easier. Unfortunately, these databases are often targeted by hackers. Protect your information by always declining the auto-save feature.

Use a fire safe: At work and at home, keep important files, unused credit cards, data CDs/DVDs, and other sensitive materials in a fire safe capable of withstanding extreme heat and water hazards for a minimum of one hour. A quality fire safe can be purchased from many reputable home-improvement centers or major retail stores (but be prepared to spend a few hundred dollars).

- **Place the safe in an inconspicuous location:** The best way to protect the safe from burglars is to keep it out of sight.

- **Bolt it to the floor or wall:** If the safe isn't anchored to a solid structure, one or two able-bodied thieves can simply carry it away and break into it later by using state-of-the-art tools.

- **Don't leave the keys lying around:** If a burglar can find the keys to your safe, all he needs to do is crack your combination and he's home free. Consider keeping the keys with you at all times or install a wall-mounted key lockbox in your home or office.

- **Don't share your combination:** This may seem obvious, but you would be surprised by how many people are burglarized by someone they entrusted with the combination to their safe.

Use off-site storage: A fire safe can help to thwart burglars from stealing information about your identity, but it can't fend off serious fires, floods, or other natural disasters. To ensure that your most important documents and valuables have the utmost protection, store them in a secure off-site location such as a safe-deposit box at your bank. Items commonly stored off-site include birth certificates, social-security cards, mortgage/loan papers, CDs/DVDs containing crucial data, jewelry, and so on.

Lock all filing cabinets: If you use filing cabinets to store important papers such as credit-card statements, bank statements, and investments transactions, then lock the cabinet to deter burglars from stealing those documents and using the information to commit identity theft. A word to the wise: Even a strong, metal filing cabinet that has been securely locked can still be broken into, so consider storing your most important papers off-site.

Check your credit report: At least once or twice a year, you should view your credit report to check for fraud, incorrect information, and other errors. Your credit history is crucial to your ability to get loans or a job (increasingly employers are using it to screen candidates), so make sure it is accurate. As of January 2005, all Americans are eligible for one free credit report per year. For more information, visit www.annualcreditreport.com.

Sign up with a credit-monitoring service: One of the best ways to fight identity theft is to sign up with a real-time credit-monitoring service from one of the three credit bureaus: Equifax, Experian, and TransUnion. This service alerts you when changes or additions are made to your credit report, which enables you to reduce the damage of credit fraud and helps you to recover more quickly. Typically, this service has a monthly or yearly fee and comes with insurance to compensate you in the event that you lose money because of identity theft or fraud.

Use photo-ID credit cards: Many financial institutions give their customers the option to have a small photo of themselves printed on their credit/debit cards. By using this service, you make it more difficult for a thief to use your stolen credit card for large purchases at retail stores. As an added bonus, it saves you from the hassle of digging through your wallet in search of your driver's license every time a store clerk asks to see your ID.

Shred sensitive documents: A determined criminal will not hesitate to rummage through your trash to look for pieces of paper or CD/DVD discs that contain private information. Protect yourself by using a cross-cut shredder to chew up your unwanted papers and discs into tiny pieces.

Opt out: Are you constantly bombarded with offers for new credit cards? Do you just toss them in the trash? Big mistake. Anyone rummaging through your trash can pull them out, mail them in, and receive a credit card in your name. Make a habit of shredding these offers before disposing of them. To opt out of receiving credit-card offers and remove your name from the credit bureaus' marketing lists, call 1-888-5OPT-OUT.

Say "No" to convenience checks: Many credit-card companies automatically send their customers special low-interest-rate "convenience checks" that can be used to make purchases or pay bills just like regular checks. Despite their alleged convenience, these checks can be a liability if they are stolen or accidentally mailed to the wrong address. Protect yourself by calling the phone number listed on the back of your credit card and insisting that the checks be stopped.

Scan your wallet: Make photocopies of all important items in your wallet, including your driver's license and all credit cards (scan their backs as well as their fronts). That way, if your wallet is ever lost or stolen, you can look at the photocopies and find the phone numbers to call to cancel your cards. Don't forget to protect the photocopies from burglars by storing them in your fire safe or in a safe-deposit box at your bank.

Surf Anonymously

Here is an unsettling fact: When you surf the Internet, your Web browser broadcasts heaps of information about your computer, including your IP address, your physical location, and numerous details about your operating system. The potential exists for online marketers and advertisers to use this information to send you targeted advertisements or for hackers to acquire details about your system to aid them in their attacks. To have complete anonymity when using the Internet, consider using an anonymous Internet provider:

- The Anonymizer (www.anonymizer.com)
- Secure Tunnel (www.secure-tunnel.com)
- iPrive.com (www.iprive.com)

- Bypass Proxy Client (www.bypass.cc)
- GhostSurf Platinum (www.tenebril.com)

Guard Your Identity

Have you ever entered a sweepstakes that required you to provide your e-mail address, name, home address, telephone number, or other information about you and your family? Did you read its rules—especially the fine print? The majority of online sweepstakes are used to gather data about you so companies can send you advertisements, special offers, and other marketing materials. To make matters worse, sometimes these companies even sell your data to third-party marketers who send you junk mail or spam. Fortunately, there are ways to reduce this annoyance and to protect your privacy:

- Do not enter contests or sweepstakes, especially those sponsored by Web sites.

- Do not give out your e-mail address to Web sites unless absolutely necessary (such as online purchases, online banking, and similar activities).

- Create a separate e-mail account for Internet purposes. That way, if you are required to divulge your e-mail address, only your junk account will be bombarded with spam.

- Never give out your social security number over the Internet.

- If possible, use fake names and fake e-mail addresses when filling out unimportant Web forms. You shouldn't do this when making online purchases or when doing Internet activity that requires your legitimate information. However, it can come in handy when a Web site asks for your e-mail address before permitting you to download a free trial version of software, or asks for your information before allowing you to view special Web content (such as movie clips).

If You Are a Victim of Identity Theft

Take immediate action by placing phone calls to the three credit bureaus. Then, send follow-up letters to them by certified mail with return receipts (which gives you proof that the bureaus received your letters). These steps should also be followed if you lose IDs or credit cards because proactive effort on your part can stop potential identity theft dead in its tracks.

1. **Put a fraud alert on your credit reports:** This prevents criminals from using your name to open new accounts, and it entitles you to free copies of your credit reports. It doesn't matter which of the three credit bureaus you call because they are required to share fraud alerts with one another.

Equifax

Web site: www.equifax.com

Phone: (800) 525-6285

Address: P.O. Box 740241, Atlanta, GA
30374-0241

Experian

Web site: www.experian.com

Phone: (888) 397-3742

Address: P.O. Box 9532, Allen, TX 75013

TransUnion

Web site: www.transunion.com

Phone: (800) 680-7289

Address: Fraud Victim Assistance Division, P.O.
Box 6790, Fullerton, CA 92834-6790

2. **Close your accounts:** Call your banks, credit-card companies, and other financial institutions to inform them of the situation. Ask for your accounts to be closed, and then follow up with a letter. For credit-card fraud, ask for fraud-dispute forms or an ID Theft Affidavit. Also, create new personal identification numbers (PINs) for all new accounts you open. For check-based fraud, ask your bank to notify the appropriate check-verification service.

3. **File a Police Report:** This might help authorities to catch the criminal, but, more important, it provides you with legitimate files to present to your creditors in case they don't believe your claims.

4. **Contact the FTC:** By filing a complaint with the Federal Trade Commission, you can provide helpful information that will enable them to fight identity theft more effectively.

Web site: http://www.consumer.gov/idtheft

Phone: (877) 438-4338

Address: Identity Theft Clearinghouse, Federal Trade
Commission, 600 Pennsylvania Avenue, NW, Washington,
DC 205800

FYI

On June 1, 2005, a new identity-theft law was enacted as part of the Accurate Credit Transaction Act. The law requires American employers to destroy information about their employees before throwing it away. Failure to comply can result in a lawsuit and/or a monetary fine. Proper destruction includes shredding or burning paper documents and wiping or smashing computer discs. This applies to all employers, even if they have only one employee. That means anyone who has a nanny, housekeeper, or gardener must abide by the law.

The Cost of Identity Theft

The Federal Trade Commission (FTC) tracks the number of identity theft and fraud cases recorded by American consumers each year—along with the estimated cost to victims in money and time—and regularly publicizes this information:

- In 2003, consumers spent nearly 300 million hours resolving their identity-theft problems.

- Between 2002 and 2004, the amount of fraud related to electronic fund transfers more than doubled.

- In 2004, identity theft and fraud cost consumers more than $547 million.

- Year after year, the most reported form of identity theft continues to be credit-card fraud.

GLOSSARY

back up: The process of copying your computer data onto CDs, DVDs, cassettes, thumbdrives, or secondary hard drives in order to protect that data from being damaged, destroyed, or stolen.

BIOS: The digital brain of your computer that controls and regulates your system. By changing the settings in the BIOS, you can alter or enhance your computer's performance.

bookmark: A shortcut used by Internet browsers to go directly to a Web site.

cable/DSL modem: A device used to provide a computer with high-speed Internet access offered by a local cable company or phone company.

chat room: An Internet meeting place where people can send and receive messages about common topics of interest. Many sexual predators and similar criminals use chat rooms to meet and solicit children.

cookie: A small text file that stores information about the Web sites you have visited and the things you did on those sites.

e-merchant: An Internet-based store or retailer that sells goods or services.

encryption: The process of transforming your data into a secret code that can be viewed only by people with the correct password. With the crime of identity theft growing worse each year, encryption has become a vital part of protecting your computer from high-tech criminals.

favorite: Another name for an Internet bookmark.

Firefox: A free Internet browser that has gained popularity as a replacement for Microsoft's Internet Explorer browser. Visit www.mozilla.org/products/firefox to download it.

firewall: A piece of hardware or software that hides your computer from the watchful eyes of online criminals, filters the data that enters your computer, controls Internet cookies, and warns you when sinister spyware programs try to transmit data about you over the Web.

hacker: The term given by the news media to people who use technology to access or break into private computers, networks, or related devices.

hard drive: The device inside your computer that stores your operating system, software, and files.

identity theft: A rapidly growing crime in which a victim's name, social security number, and other private information are stolen by a criminal and used to make fraudulent purchases, acquire bogus credit cards, and so on.

instant message: A simple text message sent from one person to another via special instant-messaging programs (such as MSN Messenger, AOL Instant Messenger, and Yahoo! Messenger).

Outlook: A popular program used to send and receive e-mail. Outlook is part of the Microsoft Office software suite, which must be purchased separately from Windows.

Outlook Express: A free program built into Windows that can send and receive e-mail.

phishing: Pronounced "fishing," this Internet scam tricks people into revealing their private, personal information (such as credit-card numbers and passwords).

pop-up: An Internet advertisement that suddenly appears in the middle of your computer screen as you browse a Web site. Some pop-ups can be carriers of spyware or other digital threats.

RAID: In a Redundant Array of Independent Disks (or RAID for short), two identical hard drives are used inside a computer. Each hard drive is a clone of the other, having the exact same operating system and programs configured in the exact same way. Not only will a RAID allow you to use certain programs and files faster (especially video-editing software), but it also protects you from a hard-drive crash by allowing you to use the clone to continue operating your computer (and, mostly important, no data is lost).

router: A device used to connect computers for the purpose of sharing files and/or an Internet connection. Many routers also have a firewall built into them to protect against Internet attacks.

spam: Annoying, troublesome — and even dangerous — unsolicited e-mail advertisements.

spyware: A general term describing dangerous programs that sneak into your computer by tricking you into installing them or by hiding in other programs you install.

steganography: A method of protecting data that allows you to hide your files in the empty space of digital photos, digital music, and more. Those pictures or songs can be viewed or played normally, and no one but you will ever know there is more than meets the eye. Typically, steganography is used to supplement encryption rather than replace it, but it can be a great alternative if you cannot or do not use encryption.

virus: A small program that is injected into your computer when you open or run an infected file. A virus can cause your computer to crash, freeze, or run slowly, and some viruses can even damage or delete your computer data.

Web browser: A program used to browse or "surf" the Internet.

Wi-Fi hacking: A term used to describe how criminals armed with wireless-enabled laptop computers will drive through neighborhoods and business parks to see if they can access unprotected and unencrypted wireless computer networks. If the criminals are successful in accessing the wireless networks, they can hijack the Internet connections to send spam or download illegal materials, view the private data on the victims' network (financial documents, credit-card numbers, social security numbers, and so on) and use that information to commit identity fraud.

worm: A program that infects a computer either by slipping into a PC that hasn't been updated with the latest security patches for Windows or by being launched when an infected e-mail attachment is opened or run. In some cases, all you have to do to become infected is to access the Internet with a computer that lacks the latest Windows security patches.

zombie: Also known as a "drone." A computer that has been hijacked by an Internet criminal. Zombies can be used to infect other computers and attack Web sites with the intention of crashing them.

INDEX

A

accessing BIOS, 138
account
    administrator, renaming, 17–19
    closing after identity theft, 184
    e-mail, using multiple, 86, 183
    Guest, disabling, 19–20
    limited, for children, creating,
        123–124
    virtual, for e-shopping, 122
    Windows, creating password for,
        135–136, 177
Accurate Credit Transaction Act, 184
administrator account, renaming,
    17–19
Advanced Attributes window, 154,
    156
Advanced Privacy Settings window,
    108
Advanced tab
    Content Advisor, 127
    Internet Options, 109–110
allowing automatic software
    installation, 10
Amazon.com, fake e-mail from, 81
anonymously surfing Web, 182–183
anti-phishing toolbar, 77
anti-spam software, 86
anti-spyware program
    cookie and, 93
    using, 69–70
antivirus software
    for cell phone, 74
    infection, actions to take for,
        62–63
    scanning with, 62
    updating, 61
    Web sites, 60–61
AOL, fake e-mail from, 81
Approved Sites tab (Content
    Advisor), 126
attachment
    to instant message, 117
    viewing blocked e-mail, 49–50

attachment alerts, enabling in
    Outlook, 56
auto log-on
    avoiding, 173, 180
    disabling, 73
    instant messaging and, 118
AutoComplete, disabling, 107–108,
    173
automatic dialing, 68
Automatic Updates tab (System
    Properties dialog box), 7
automatically allowing software
    installation, 10
automatically updating Windows, 6–7
auto-save of credit information,
    avoiding, 180
avoiding
    auto log-on, 173, 180
    auto-save of credit information,
        180
    convenience check, 182
    obvious password, 139
    phishing, 76–77
    private chat, 119

B

backing up data
    copying data to device, 166–167
    devices for, 164–166
    disc image, creating, 168
    frequency of, 164
    laptop and, 178
    manually, 167
    reasons for, 163–164
    storage of, 168–169
Bank of America, fake e-mail from, 80
battery backup, 169
BIOS password, creating, 137–138,
    177
blocked e-mail attachment, viewing,
    49–50
blocking
    cookies, 108–109
    pop-up windows, 101

Continued

blocking, *(continued)*
    strangers from IM, 117, 118
    Web sites and content, 124–128
blog, 86
Bluetooth technology, 74
bookmarking Web site, 6, 67
brownout, 169
browser. *See also* Firefox Web browser; Internet
    Explorer
    Opera, 102
    options for, 102
    pop-up blocker and, 101
burning software, 168

C

cable/DSL modem, 187
case, conspicuous, for laptop computer, 178
CD burner, recordable or rewriteable, 165–166
CD, disposing of, 152
cell phone, data snatching by, 74
cell-phone Internet, 73
Certificate screen, General tab, 79
chat room
    children and, 129
    safety in, 119
checking account, protecting, 121–122
children
    backing up data and, 164
    blocking Web sites and content from,
        124–128
    chatting and, 129
    instant messaging and, 129
    Internet history of, viewing, 128–129
    limited account for, creating, 123–124
clearing
    history, 174–175
    Pagefile, 25–27
closing pop-up ad, 69
Comcast, fake e-mail from, 80
complaint, filing with Federal Trade
    Commission, 184
computer
    donating or selling, 150
    laptop, protecting, 177–178
    locking, 14
    public, using, 173–175
    shredding data from, 150, 151
    theft of, 164, 177–178
    zombie or drone, 64
Computer Management screen
    creating password, 136
    removing "Password is About to Expire"
        notice, 144
    renaming administrator account, 18, 19, 20
Configuration tab (Network screen), 24

Confirm Attribute Changes dialog box, 156, 159
contact/buddy list for instant messaging, 117, 118
Content Advisor feature (Internet Explorer),
    124–127
content, blocking from children, 124–128
Content tab (Internet Options dialog box),
    107, 125
contest, entering, 183
convenience check, avoiding, 182
cookie
    blocking, 108–109
    browser tweaks for, 89–91
    deleting, 174
    description of, 87
    manually deleting, 88–89
    software solutions for, 93
    tracking, 87–88
    trustworthy, 87
Cookie Crusher program, 93
copying data to backup device, 166–167
credit bureaus, 184
credit card, photo-ID, 182
credit report
    checking, 181
    fraud alert on, 183
credit-monitoring service, 181
cross-site scripting, 76

D

data, backing up
    copying data to device, 166–167
    devices for, 164–166
    disc image, creating, 168
    frequency of, 164
    laptop and, 178
    manually, 167–168
    reasons for, 163–164
    storage of, 168–169
debit card, 121
deleting
    cookie, 88–89, 174
    file, 149
    spam, 85
DHCP, disabling, 73
disabling
    auto log-on, 73
    AutoComplete, 107–108, 173
    DHCP, 73
    Dump File, 27–28
    File and Printer Sharing, 23–24
    Guest account, 19–20
    Messenger, 40–41
    Preview pane
        in Outlook, 51–52
        in Outlook Express, 46–47
        for virus and worm protection, 65–66

remote administration, 100
Remote Assistance, 22–23
Remote Desktop, 20–22
Simple File Sharing, 28–29
VBScripts, 36–39
Welcome Screen, 14, 133–134
disaster, natural, 164
disc image, creating, 168
disposing
of CD, DVD, floppy, or zip disk, 152
of computer hardware, 152
of hard drive, 151–152
donating computer, 150
downloading security patch or service pack, 51
drone computer, 64
Dump File, disabling, 27–28
DVD
disposing of, 152
dual-layer, 165
DVD burner, recordable or rewriteable, 165–166

E

EarthLink, fake e-mail from, 82
eBay, fake e-mail from, 80
Edit DWORD Value dialog box, 27
Edit File Type dialog box, 39
Edit String dialog box, 16, 17
editing Registry
Pagefile, clearing, 25–27
reading e-mail in plain text in Outlook, 53–55
screensaver hack, preventing, 14–17
special extensions, unhiding, 35–36
e-mail
address, giving out, 183
multiple accounts, using, 86, 183
phishing
avoiding, 76–77
description of, 75
spotting fake e-mail, 79–83
types of, 75–76
warning signs of, 76
reading in plain text
in Outlook, 52–55
in Outlook Express, 48
sending in plain text
in Outlook, 55
in Outlook Express, 49
spam
description of, 85
strategies for dealing with, 85–86
spotting fake, 79–83
unsecure, 73
viewing safely
in Outlook, 52
in Outlook Express, 47–48

e-mail phishing, 75
e-merchant, 187
enabling
attachment alerts in Outlook, 56
maximum security on Outlook Express,
45–46
encryption
description of, 153
of file, 154–155
of folder, 155–157
identity theft and, 180
laptop and, 178
of Offline Files, 160
software programs, 153–154
of Temp folder, 158–159
wireless device and, 72
wireless keyboard and, 74
Encryption Warning dialog box, 155
engraving name on laptop, 178
Equifax credit bureau, 184
erasing tracks on public computer, 174
e-shopping, strategies for, 121–122
evil twin hotspot, 73
Exceptions dialog box (Firefox Web browser),
92, 114
Experian credit bureau, 184

F

fake information, giving to Web site, 183
Favorites, adding to, 6
Federal Trade Commission (FTC) filing
complaint with, 184
file
deleting, 149
encrypting, 154–155
manually backing up, 167–168
File and Printer Sharing, disabling, 23–24
file cabinet, locking, 181
file extensions, unhiding, 34–35
File Types tab (Folder Options dialog box), 37
fire safe, 169, 180–181
Firefox Web browser
cookie, tweaks for, 91–92
deleting cookie, 89
description of, 102
history, viewing, 128
security settings, configuring, 110–115
firewall
cookie and, 93
description of, 97
hardware, 98
software, 98–99
testing, 101
types of, 98

firmware
  for router, 100
  for Wi-Fi, 72
floppy disk, disposing of, 152
folder
  encrypting, 155–157
  making private, 145–148
  Temp, encrypting, 158–159
Folder Options dialog box
  File Types tab, 37
  Offline Files tab, 160
  View tab, 29, 35, 148
FTC (Federal Trade Commission) filing
  complaint with, 184

G

General tab
  Certificate screen, 79
  Content Advisor, 126
  Internet Options, 88, 174
  Local Area Connection Properties, 24
  Messenger Properties, 41
  Properties dialog box, 145
Guest account, disabling, 19–20

H

hacker, 188
hard drive
  corrupt or damaged, 163
  disposing of, 151–152
  external, and backing up data, 164–165
  internal, and backing up data, 165
  lifespan of, 168
  unplugging during storm, 169
  wiping, 151
hardware
  disposing of, 152
  password-protection features of, accessing,
    138
hardware firewall, 98
Hidden Folder Properties dialog box, 147
history, clearing, 174–175
home page hijacking, 67, 68
hosts file, modifying, 31–34
hotspot, evil twin, 73

I

icons
  padlock, 77–78
  Recycle Bin, 149
ICS (Internet Connection Sharing), 100
identity, guarding
  chat room and, 119
  instant messaging and, 117

identity theft
  actions for victim of, 183–184
  cost of, 184–185
  encryption and, 153
  e-shopping and, 121
  password and, 140
  strategies for thwarting, 179–182
IIS (Internet Information Services), disabling,
  29–30
instant messaging (IM)
  children and, 129
  strategies for handling, 117–118
instant-message phishing, 75
Internet Connection Sharing (ICS), 100
Internet Explorer
  Advanced Options, configuring, 109–110
  alternatives to, 102
  AutoComplete, disabling, 107–108
  Content Advisor feature, 124–127
  cookie
    blocking, 108–109
    deleting, 88–89
    tweaks for, 89–91
  History button, 128
  security level
    custom, creating, 103–104
    default, choosing, 104–105
    trusted sites, adding, 105–107
Internet history, viewing, 128–129
Internet Information Services (IIS), disabling,
  29–30
Internet Options
  Advanced tab, 109–110
  Content tab, 107, 125
  General tab, 88, 174
  Security tab, 105, 106
Internet service provider (ISP)
  anonymous, 182–183
  content filtering and, 128
  spam filter of, 86
Internet Tools dialog box, 30

K

keyboard, wireless, 74
keys to fire safe, 181
keystroke logging, 64, 68, 173

L

laptop computer, protecting, 177–178
limited account for children, creating, 123–124
links
  in e-mail
    phishing and, 75, 76, 79
    spam and, 86
  in instant message, 76, 77, 117

Local Area Connection Properties, General
 tab, 24
locking
 computer, 14
 file cabinet, 181
logging off
 importance of, 180
 instant messaging session, 73
 public computer, 174
 when leaving computer, 13
logging on. *See also* auto log-on
 automatic, avoiding, 173, 180
 secure, requiring, 134–135

M

MAC Address Filtering, 73
macro virus, 61–62
manually backing up data, 167–168
manually deleting cookie, 88–89
manually updating Windows, 3–5
maximum security on Outlook Express, enabling,
 45–46
meeting person from chat room, 119
message, posting on Internet, 86
Messenger, disabling, 40–41
Messenger Properties dialog box, General tab, 41
Microsoft
 fake e-mail from, 79–80
 fake security bulletins, 82–83
 Office, updating, 7–12, 97
 Windows
  account, creating password for, 177
  updating automatically, 6–7, 97
  updating manually, 3–5
 Windows Encryption
  file, encrypting, 154–155
  folder, encrypting, 155–157
  permission, granting, 157
 Windows Firewall, 98–99
 Windows XP
  Service Pack 2 and, 45, 98–99
  System Restore feature, 147
modem, cable/DSL, 187
modifying hosts file, 31–34
motherboard, BIOS password for, 137–138
MSN, fake e-mail from, 81
multi-format DVD burner, 165

N

Network screen, Configuration tab, 24
New Folder Properties dialog box, Sharing tab,
 146
nickname, choosing for chat room, 119
Notepad, hosts file in, 32–33, 34

O

Office (Microsoft), updating, 8–12, 97
Offline Files, encrypting, 160
off-site storage of data, 169, 181
Open With dialog box, 32
opening spam, 85
Opera Web browser, 102
Options dialog box
 Firefox Web browser
  Advanced, 115
  General, 111
  Privacy, 89, 92, 111, 112, 113
  Web Features, 114
 Outlook Express
  Read tab, 48
  Security tab, 46
  Send tab, 49
Outlook Express, protecting
 blocked e-mail attachment, viewing, 49–50
 maximum security, enabling, 45–46
 Preview pane, disabling, 46–47
 reading e-mail in plain text, 48
 sending e-mail in plain text, 49
 Service Pack 2 and, 45
 viewing e-mail, 47–48
Outlook, protecting
 attachment alerts, turning on, 56
 e-mail details, viewing safely, 52
 Preview pane, disabling, 51–52
 reading e-mail in plain text, 52–55
 security patches and service packs,
  downloading, 51
 sending e-mail in plain text, 55

P

padlock icon, 77–78, 121
Pagefile, clearing, 25–27
passphrase, 139
password
 AutoComplete, disabling, 107–108
 for BIOS, creating, 137–138, 177
 for children, creating, 127
 forgetting primary, 142–143
 for hardware, changing, 138
 new, creating, and previously encrypted files
  and e-mail, 143
 obvious, avoiding, 139
 protecting, 148
 remembering, 140
 for router, 100
 for screensaver, requiring, 137
 strong, using, 138–139, 177
 System Restore feature and, 147
 unique, using, 179

Continued

password *(continued)*
for Web site, 140, 179
for Windows account, creating, 135–136, 177
for wireless device, 72
"Password is About to Expire" notice, removing, 143–145
password-recovery software, 148
password-reset disk
creating, 140–141
using, 141–142
PayPal, fake e-mail from, 81
Per Site Privacy Actions screen, 91
permission to view encrypted data, granting, 157
Personal Web server, disabling, 29–30
pharming, 75
phishing
avoiding, 76–77
description of, 75
spotting fake e-mail, 79–83
types of, 75–76
warning signs of, 76
photo-ID credit card, 182
plain text
reading e-mail in, in Outlook Express, 48
sending e-mail in
in Outlook, 55
in Outlook Express, 49
police report, filing after identity theft, 184
pop-up windows
blocking, 101
spyware and, 67, 69
posting message on Internet, 86
power surge, 163, 169
preventing screensaver hack, 14–17
Preview pane, disabling
in Outlook, 51–52
in Outlook Express, 46–47
spam and, 86
for virus and worm protection, 65–66
private chat, avoiding, 119
private information, protecting, 180, 183
private, making folder, 145–148
Properties dialog box
General tab, 145
Sharing tab, 145–146
protecting. *See also* Outlook Express, protecting; Outlook, protecting
checking account, 121–122
laptop computer, 177–178
password, 148
private information, 180, 183
public computer, strategies for using, 173–175

R

RAID (Redundant Array of Independent Discs), 166
Ratings tab (Content Advisor), 125
Read tab (Options dialog box, Outlook Express), 48
reading e-mail
offline, 76
in plain text
in Outlook, 52–55
in Outlook Express, 48
Recycle Bin
deleting file from, 149–150
restoring file from, 149
Recycle Bin icon, 149
Redundant Array of Independent Discs (RAID), 166
Registry, editing
Pagefile, clearing, 25–27
reading e-mail in plain text in Outlook, 53–55
screensaver hack, preventing, 14–17
special extensions, unhiding, 35–36
remote administration, disabling for router, 100
Remote Assistance, disabling, 22–23
Remote Desktop, disabling, 20–22
Remote tab (System Properties dialog box), 21, 23
removing
"Password is About to Expire" notice, 143–145
Web server, 29–30
renaming administrator account, 17–19
restoring file from Recycle Bin, 149
router
brands of, 98
securing, 100
Run dialog box, 15, 143

S

scanning important information, 182
screensaver
hack of, preventing, 14–17
requiring password for, 137
secure logon, requiring, 134–135
security certificate, checking, 77–79
security level
custom, creating, 103–104
default, choosing, 104–105
security measures
Dump File, disabling, 27–28
File and Printer Sharing, disabling, 23–24
file extensions, unhiding, 34–35
Guest account, disabling, 19–20
hosts file, modifying, 31–34
Messenger, disabling, 40–41

Outlook
   attachment alerts, turning on, 56
   e-mail details, viewing safely, 52
   Preview pane, disabling, 51–52
   reading e-mail in plain text, 52–55
   security patches and service packs,
      downloading, 51
   sending e-mail in plain text, 55
Outlook Express
   blocked e-mail attachment, viewing,
      49–50
   e-mail, viewing safely, 47–48
   maximum security, enabling, 45–46
   Preview pane, disabling, 46–47
   reading e-mail in plain text, 48
   sending e-mail in plain text, 49
Pagefile, clearing, 25–27
Remote Assistance, disabling, 22–23
Remote Desktop, disabling, 20–22
renaming administrator account, 17–19
screensaver hack, preventing, 14–17
Simple File Sharing, disabling, 28–29
special extensions, unhiding, 35–36
temporary
   locking computer, 14
   logging off, 13
VBScripts, disabling, 36–39
Web server, removing, 29–30
for wireless device, 72
Security screen, Security Level tab, 62
Security Settings window, 103
Security tab
   Internet Options dialog box, 105, 106
   Options dialog box (Outlook Express), 46
Select User window, 157
selling computer, 150
Send tab (Options dialog box, Outlook Express),
   49
sending e-mail in plain text
   in Outlook, 55
   in Outlook Express, 49
serial number of laptop, 178
service pack, 5, 10
Service Pack 2 (Windows XP)
   security features and, 45
   Windows Firewall and, 98–99
Services screen, 41
Sharing tab (Properties dialog box), 145–146
shopping online, strategies for, 121–122
shortcut to Web site, creating, 6
shredding
   data from computer, 150, 151
   documents, 182
Simple File Sharing, disabling, 28–29
social security number, protecting, 180

software
   allowing automatic installation of, 10
   anti-spam, 86
   anti-spyware, 69–70, 93
   antivirus software
      for cell phone, 74
      infection, actions to take for, 62–63
      scanning with, 62
      updating, 61
      Web sites, 60–61
   browser and, 102
   burning, 168
   content-filtering, 127
   for cookie solutions, 93
   disc-imaging, 168
   drive-wiping, 151
   encryption, 153–154
   firewall, 98–99
   password-recovery, 148
   steganography, 161
   tracking, 178
   "vault", 140
   wiping, 150
spam
   description of, 85
   strategies for dealing with, 85–86
special extensions, unhiding, 35–36
spim, 118
spotting fake e-mail, 79–83
spyware
   dealing with, 69–70
   description of, 67
   operation of, 68–69
   symptoms of, 67–68
SSID, 72–73
Startup and Recovery screen, 28
steganography software, 161
storing backup data, 168–169
storm, unplugging hard drive during, 169
strong password, using, 138–139, 177
surfing Web
   anonymously, 182–183
   caution when, 100–101
surge protector, 169
sweepstakes, entering, 183
System Properties
   Automatic Updates tab, 7
   Remote tab, 21, 23
System Restore feature (Windows XP), 147

T

tape drive, 166
telephone phishing, 76, 77
Temp folder, encrypting, 158–159

temporary security measures
  locking computer, 14
  logging off, 13
testing firewall, 101
theft of computer
  backing up data and, 164
  laptop, 177–178
toolbars
  anti-phishing, 77
  blocking pop-up windows with, 101
  uninvited, 68
tracking software, 178
tracks, erasing, 174
TransUnion credit bureau, 184
Trojan horse, 59
trusted site, adding, 105–107
Trusted sites window, 106

U

unhiding
  file extensions, 34–35
  special extensions, 35–36
Uninterruptible Power Supply, 169
unplugging hard drive during storm, 169
updating
  antivirus software, 61
  Microsoft Office, 7–12, 97
  Windows
    automatically, 6–7
    importance of, 97
    manually, 3–5
URL hijacking, 76
USB thumbdrive, 166
UseNet, 86
User Accounts screen, 20, 124, 134, 141

V

VBScripts, disabling, 36–39
View tab (Folder Options dialog box), 29, 35, 148
viewing
  blocked e-mail attachment in Outlook Express, 49–50
  e-mail details in Outlook, 52
  e-mail in Outlook Express, 47–48
  encrypted data, permission for, 157
  Internet history, 128–129
virtual account number for e-shopping, 122
virtual memory, clearing, 25–27
virus
  backing up data and, 163
  damage from, 61
  description of, 59, 64
  infection, actions to take for, 62–64
  macro, protection from, 61–62
  protection from, 60

  scanning for, 62
  symptoms of, 59
Visa, fake e-mail from, 81

W

wallet, information in, scanning, 182
Web browser. *See also* Firefox Web browser; Internet Explorer
  Opera, 102
  options for, 102
  pop-up blocker and, 101
Web server, removing, 29–30
Web sites
  anti-phishing toolbars, 77
  anti-spam software, 86
  anti-spyware programs, 70
  antivirus software, 60–61
  blocking, 124–128
  bookmarking, 6, 67
  burning software, 168
  caution when surfing, 100–101
  content-filtering software, 127
  cookie programs, 93
  credit bureaus, 184
  credit report, 181
  disc-imaging programs, 168
  drive-wiping software, 151
  encryption software, 154
  Federal Trade Commission, 184
  Firefox Web browser, 102
  firewall testing, 101
  firewalls, 99
  Office Update, 8–12
  Opera Web browser, 102
  password for, 140, 179
  security certificate, checking, 77–79
  shortcuts to, creating, 6
  steganography software, 161
  surfing anonymously, 182–183
  toolbars, 101
  tracking software, 178
  Windows Update, 3–5
  wiping software, 150
Welcome Screen, disabling, 14, 133–134
Wi-Fi hacking, 71–73
Window Layout Properties screen, 47
Window Washer program, 93
Windows
  account, creating password for, 177
  updating automatically, 6–7, 97
  updating manually, 3–5
Windows Components Wizard, 30
Windows Encryption
  file, encrypting, 154–155
  folder, encrypting, 155–157
  permission, granting, 157

Windows Firewall, 98–99
Windows XP
 Service Pack 2 and, 45, 98–99
 System Restore feature, 147
wiping data from computer, 150, 151
wireless devices
 hacking and, 71–73
 hotspots and, 73
wireless keyboard, 74
worm
 damage from, 64
 description of, 64
 prevention of, 65
 symptoms of, 59

Y

Yahoo! Toolbar, 101

Z

zip disk, disposing of, 152
zombie computer, 64
ZoneAlarm firewall, 99